A Long

Tangled Saga

THE STORY OF THE PAIRC ESTATE COMMUNITY BUYOUT

BOB CHAMBERS

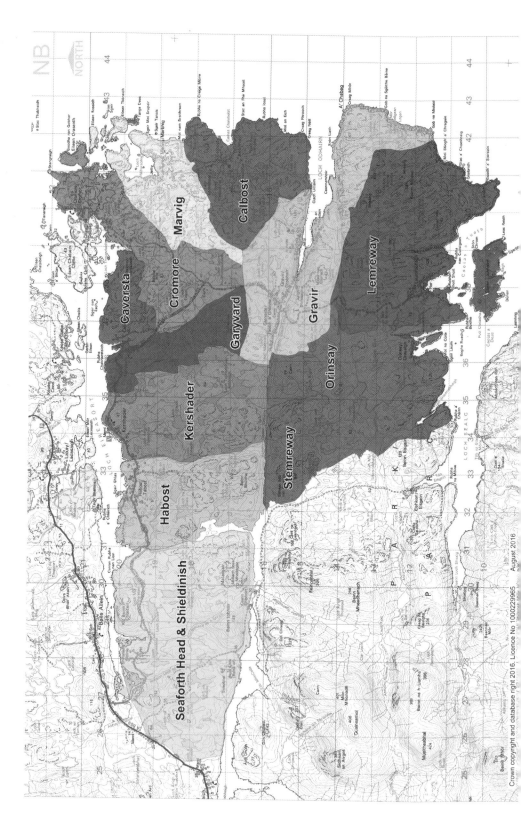

Pairc Estate and its Townships

A Long and Tangled Saga

THE STORY OF THE PAIRC ESTATE COMMUNITY BUYOUT

BOB CHAMBERS

First published in 2021 by Acair,
An Tosgan, Seaforth Road, Stornoway, Isle of Lewis, HS1 2SD

www.acairbooks.com
info@acairbooks.com

Text © Dr Bob Chambers, 2021
Original artworks © Fiona Rennie (Sradag Creative) for Acair.

Text and cover design by Fiona Rennie (Sradag Creative) for Acair
Main cover image © Jan Schouten
Back cover image © Donnie Morrison
Author image © Melanie Ritchie

A CIP catalogue record for this title is available from the British Library.

Printed by Hussar Books, Poland
ISBN: 978-1-78907-111-5

Scottish Charity Regulator
Registered Charity SC047866

For the People of Pairc – Past, Present and Future

This book was commissioned by the Pairc Trust in 2016

- CONTENTS -

Final Observations

- LIST OF ILLUSTRATIONS -

Plate 1. Map of Pairc Estate from the title deed of sale by Lord Leverhulme to Pairc Crofters Ltd in 1924 (Register of Sasines)

Plate 2. Map showing the approximate boundaries of Steimreway and the crofting townships of Pairc (courtesy of Comhairle nan Eilean Siar)

Plate 3. Ruins of the former village of Steimreway (courtesy of John Randall)

Plate 4. View of the village of Calbost from the south (courtesy of John Randall)

Plate 5. View of the village of Lemreway in 2006 showing hay harvested in the traditional way (courtesy of John Randall)

Plate 6. Members of the wider Pairc community at the deserted village of Steimreway in 2010 (courtesy of Donnie Morrison)

Plate 7. Residents of Pairc queuing to vote in the first community ballot in November 2004 (courtesy of Donnie Morrison)

Plate 8. Officials of Comhairle nan Eilean Siar counting the vote following the third community ballot in May 2014 (courtesy of Donnie Morrison)

Plate 9. Members of Pairc Trust at a public meeting in March 2011 (courtesy of Donnie Morrison)

Plate 10. Directors of Pairc Trust in June 2005 with Sandra Holmes of HIE (second left) (courtesy of Donnie Morrison)

Plate 11. Map of Pairc Estate showing approximate boundaries as purchased by Pairc Trust in December 2015 (updated and adapted from map prepared by Registers of Scotland for Pairc Trust dated September 2014)

Plate 12. Alasdair Allan MSP and Angus McDowall in July 2016 unveiling the plaque to mark the completion of the buyout (courtesy of Donnie Morrison)

- FOREWORD -

Bob Chambers has written a painstakingly researched and well put-together account of how people in the Pairc area of Lewis managed to obtain ownership of the estate on which they live. At one level, the pages that follow constitute a factual record of what these people did. At another, these same pages are a tribute to this island community's remarkable tenacity. When Pairc residents set out to gain possession of the land around them, the task was expected to be fairly straightforward. It proved to be anything but. The Land Reform Act of 2003, seen widely as one of the more significant pieces of legislation to be passed by Scotland's devolved parliament, had given communities like Pairc's new purchase rights. But those rights, Pairc people discovered, were by no means easy to exercise. The innumerable obstacles and complexities they encountered were so difficult and time-consuming to surmount or get through that it would have been perfectly understandable if Pairc's land ownership ambitions had eventually been abandoned. But this did not happen. Month after month, year after year, the Pairc community stuck with a process that, as Bob Chambers demonstrates, embroiled community leaders in hugely protracted and energy-sapping dealings with public agencies, civil servants, politicians, lawyers, the previous owner and others. That took a great deal of commitment on the part of everyone involved. More than anything else, it was this commitment to attaining their ownership objectives that at last put Pairc people in charge of their own place. Pairc's future prospects, as a result, are much brighter than they might have been. But something else has been accomplished as well. A long, long story of exploitation and injustice has been provided, in Pairc at least, with a most satisfactory conclusion.

This story began in the 1820s and 1830s when Pairc's then owner, James Stewart MacKenzie, proprietor of all of Lewis, was looking to cash in, as many other Highlands and Islands lairds were already doing, on early nineteenth-century Britain's almost insatiable demand for the wool needed to clothe the country's rapidly expanding population. At this time, as MacKenzie's factor remarked contentedly, sheep farming tenants 'could be got as fast as the lands could be cleared for them'. Particularly attractive to such tenants were upland grazings of the sort that were a feature of the hilly peninsula lying between Loch Erisort and Loch Seaforth in Lewis's south-eastern corner. Much of this peninsula, all of it then known as Pairc, was duly emptied of its inhabitants. Many of the people thus turned out of homes and landholdings were moved to other parts of Lewis where they were settled on already existing (but subdivided) crofts or on entirely new crofts created for them by the simple expedient of pegging out croft boundaries on previously unoccupied bog and moorland. Not everyone evicted in the course of these clearances left Pairc, however. Some of the families evicted in the course of the 1820s and 1830s were accommodated in surviving villages or townships in the more northerly part of the peninsula. This is the area known today as the Pairc Estate – the area that's the subject of this book.

South of this area, and occupying the bulk of the wider Pairc peninsula, James Stewart MacKenzie put in place an enormous sheep farm. But this farm would itself disappear within a half-century of its creation – the sheep that had taken the place of so many families now being replaced, in their turn, by deer. From the perspective of many Lewis people struggling to survive on three or four acres or, in lots of instances, on next to no land at all, it seemed as wrong as it was galling that the Matheson family, who had bought Lewis in 1844, thought it more fitting to rent much of Pairc to a wealthy sporting tenant, a Midlands industrialist called Joseph Platt, than to make its grazings available to descendants of folk who had pastured cattle on these grazings for hundreds of years. The outcome, in November 1887, was a well-organised invasion of Pairc Deer Forest by men who, with a view to highlighting their demands for the restoration to them of land that had been depopulated, set about slaughtering as many deer as possible. Speaking to a press reporter in the days following the 'deer raid', as this episode became known, one of the young men who took part 'stated that his father's family were among those evicted' when much of Pairc was cleared. 'It is impossible,' the pressman noted of this man, 'to imagine with what intense bitterness he gave expression to the feelings with which he said he gazed upon the ruins of his grandfather's cottage.'

Anyone wishing to get to grips more fully with this history of oppression and eventual fight-back can do no better than visit the community-run archive in Pairc's Ravenspoint Centre. Angus Macleod, the man whose writings are preserved there, knew Pairc's history as few today can know it. Angus was brought up in

Calbost on the Pairc Estate and, despite being struck down by life-threatening illness when young, went on to make a big contribution to the life both of Lewis and of the Highlands and Islands more generally. My own memories of this remarkable man derive mainly from the period in the 1980s when I worked for the then newly set up Scottish Crofters Union (SCU), now the Scottish Crofting Federation. Angus, the SCU's founding father, was to me a good friend as well as a mentor. And because we shared an interest in the crofting past as well as in the crofting future, the Pairc clearances, the 1887 deer raid and all sorts of associated topics came up repeatedly in the course of the late-night and early-morning conversations that were a feature of my many stays in the home Angus shared with his wife Annie at Marybank near Stornoway.

Those conversations resurfaced in my mind when reading this book. Angus Macleod, I believe, would have taken a real delight in what has been achieved by the people Bob Chambers writes about. Angus would have been equally pleased, I think, by the way Bob handles the tale he has to tell. This is no simplistic analysis of the sort intended to give the impression that community effort of the Pairc variety is invariably characterised by solid and unshakeable unity on the community side. As Bob Chambers is clearly well aware, matters are seldom, if ever, so straightforward. This book, it follows, is the product of a determination to explore, among many other things, the tensions and disagreements that can so readily come to the fore in the context of attempts to change something as basic as the ownership structure of an entire locality. I very much welcome this approach. In today's Scotland, where more than 600,000 acres have been brought into community ownership over the last 25 or so years, the impression is sometimes given that anyone venturing down this road will find the going easy. They will not. The Pairc experience, to be sure, proved more challenging than most. But that is all the more reason to have a scrupulously detailed record of exactly what it entailed. This is what Bob Chambers has provided.

James Hunter

TIME LINE FOR THE
PAIRC ESTATE COMMUNITY BUYOUT

THE MAIN MILESTONES IN THE LONG HISTORY OF
THE PAIRC BUYOUT WERE AS FOLLOWS:

* **December 2002** – Members of the Pairc community informed about a commercial wind farm proposal on the Pairc Estate.

* **January 2003** – Pairc Community Liaison Group formed (PCLG) to represent the community in further discussions with the landlord of the Pairc Estate (Pairc Crofters Ltd) and the wind farm developer Scottish and Southern Energy (SSE).

* **December 2003** – Pairc Trust formally established with powers to pursue a community buyout.

* **November 2004** – First ballot confirms community support for an application to buy the common grazings on the Pairc Estate under Part 3 of the Land Reform (Scotland) Act 2003.

* **May 2005** – Part 3 application submitted by the Pairc Trust to Scottish Ministers to purchase the common grazings on the Pairc Estate.

* **November 2005** – Scottish Ministers refer the interposed lease set up by the landlord (between Pairc Crofters Ltd and Pairc Renewables Ltd) to the Scottish Land Court for a judgement on its validity.

* **August 2007** – Scottish Land Court finds that interposed leases are valid in a crofting context and that Crofting Community Bodies such as the Pairc Trust can purchase all of the landlord's interest in the land, burdened with the rights of third parties including rights under interposed leases – the Land Reform Act 2003 has already been amended to extend the crofting community right to buy to cover leases.

* **September 2007** – Landlord agrees to discussions with the Pairc Trust about a voluntary transfer.

* **July 2009** – Pairc Trust concludes that the landlord is delaying in the hope that the commercial wind farm project is approved and the value of the estate increased; and prepares to make new applications under Part 3 of the Act.

* **December 2009** – Second ballot approves community support for new Part 3 applications to purchase both land and the interposed lease.

* **February 2010** – New applications for purchase of the land and interposed lease under Part 3 of the Land Reform Act submitted to Scottish Government.

* **May 2010** – Landlord unsuccessfully petitions Court of Session to suspend the decision by Scottish Ministers to start consultation on the new applications.

* **March 2011** – Following consideration of comments made during the extensive statutory consultation process, Scottish Ministers formally approve the new 2010 Part 3 applications and turn down the now outdated 2005 application.

* **April 2011** – Landlord appeals to Stornoway Sheriff Court against the decision by Scottish Ministers to approve the new Part 3 applications, and the valuation process which had been started is stopped.

* **October 2011** – Landlord's appeal heard in Stornoway Sheriff Court and the first part of his case relating to the European Convention on Human Rights is referred by the Sheriff to the Court of Session. The other parts of the appeal are 'sisted' (suspended).

—* **December 2012** – Court of Session rejects first part of landlord's appeal on human rights grounds against Scottish Ministers. The other parts of the appeal remain suspended pending further discussions between the landlord and the Pairc Trust.

—* **March 2013** – Discussions between the Pairc Trust and the landlord on a voluntary transfer of the whole estate are intensified with David Cameron acting as mediator.

—* **November 2013** – Informal agreement reached by the Pairc Trust and the landlord on Non-binding Heads of Terms for a voluntary transfer of the whole estate, subject to endorsement by the community.

—* **May 2014** – Third community ballot approves Draft Offer for the Pairc Trust to purchase the land and lease based on the Heads of Terms. A funding package has been negotiated with funding bodies.

—* **May 2015** – Following further legal input, and detailed mapping of the whole estate, a legally binding Final Offer is made for the whole estate and interposed lease, and missives are formally exchanged. Date of Entry depends on settlement of the landlord's reasonable legal expenses.

—* **November 2015** – Interim Auditor makes his determination on the landlord's expenses. The funding package is updated and finalised.

—* **December 2015** – Title to the whole of Pairc Estate is formally transferred to the Pairc Trust.

- INTRODUCTION -

The Pairc Estate passed into community ownership on 4 December 2015. It was the culmination of a process that had begun almost precisely thirteen years earlier in December 2002. This was, by far, the longest time taken for the transfer of land in Scotland from private to community ownership.

The lineage of community land ownership in the Highlands and Islands can be traced back to the early part of the twentieth century in the form of the 20,000-acre Glendale Estate in north-west Skye. This was purchased by the state in 1903 by the Congested Districts Board, which then transferred ownership to the former tenants by means of fifty-year purchase agreements. That was followed in 1924 by the establishment of the Stornoway Trust in Lewis to manage 64,000 acres gifted to the community by Lord Leverhulme.

The process then came to an abrupt halt until in much more modern times the 21,000-acre North Lochinver Estate in Assynt on the north-west mainland coast was successfully bought on the open market in December 1992 by its crofting tenants in the form of the Assynt Crofters Trust. This was followed by a veritable surge in community ownership in other parts of the Highlands and Islands – with communities such as Eigg (1997), Knoydart (1999), Gigha (2002), North Harris (2003), South Uist (2006) and Galson (2007) leading the way. Part 3 of the Land Reform (Scotland) Act 2003, one of the first pieces of legislation to be passed by the new Scottish Parliament, gave crofting communities the right to apply to purchase croft land in circumstances where a landowner was unwilling to sell. However, all of the sales to date have been achieved through voluntary transfers.

The Pairc community first embarked on its long journey to acquire the local Pairc Estate in 2002 and during the subsequent thirteen years was overtaken by several other communities. Pairc has proved to be a unique case in several ways – not just for the extreme length of time taken for the change in land ownership, but also for the high degree of complexity of the processes involved. To date, Pairc is the only crofting community to have submitted a successful application to Scottish Government to purchase land using Part 3 of the Land Reform (Scotland) Act 2003 against the wishes of the landlord – even though the eventual purchase was made on a voluntary basis.

As such the story of the transfer deserves to be examined and commented upon dispassionately and independently before the details become blurred or lost with the passage of time.

The author – a writer and historian with a particular interest in the crofting history of the Hebrides – was approached by the Pairc Trust in January 2016 and invited to write an independent history of the transfer which also highlighted the lessons that might be learnt from it. The Trust did not seek to ensure that a text should be produced which reflected favourably or uncritically on itself.

The author has not received a fee from the Trust which strengthened his objectivity and independent stance. His aim is to present a fair, objective and balanced account based on the evidence as he sees it, of what became at times an acrimonious and bitterly contested conflict between the Pairc Trust and the previous owner.

Some of the details of the buyout are very complex and technical. The author has attempted to keep the text as simple and understandable as possible in relation to such issues in order that the script remains of interest to most readers, especially the general reader. Where detailed or technical explanations are considered to be necessary for the general reader, the author has attempted to keep these as short and clear as possible. Footnotes or endnotes have not been used in order to help with the flow of the text for the general reader. That should not be taken as a signal that this is not a rigorous analysis of the buyout. It is, or most certainly an attempt to be.

The author has drawn on a variety of information sources and people's opinions. In particular the Pairc Trust has been an important source especially through its written records and other documentation. In addition the author has spoken at length to a number of past and present Pairc Trust directors. Furthermore, the author has been given unfettered access to all of the Pairc Trust's various written records, documents, correspondence, notes of meetings etc.

A number of other key organisations and individuals who figure prominently in the story have also been consulted and information and opinions gathered from them. Important amongst these have been the Western Isles Council (Comhairle nan Eilean Siar – CnES), Highlands and Islands Enterprise (HIE), and Scottish Government.

Roy Shearer, now a retired partner of Lindsays solicitors who acted on behalf of the Pairc Trust on the buyout for several years, has provided invaluable documents and assistance to the author, especially concerning many complicated legal and technical matters involved during the extraordinarily lengthy period of the buyout.

A number of key people involved in the Pairc Estate buyout were contacted by the author for help with the study. This was done in a variety of ways – e mail, telephone, meetings, or being sent customised questions to answer. For written responses the author indicated that he was not looking for exhaustive text but simply a few paragraphs at the most for each question or less for some – not least to minimise the call on an individual's time. All those approached were offered the facility of their contributions being anonymous. Not all contributed, including Barry Lomas (the previous landowner) who was sent a number of written questions.

Barry Lomas requested confirmation that his response would be published in its entirety. The author replied that he expected to be able to do this provided the length of the text was consistent with the guidelines as set out above. No other caveats were specified by the author. An indication was given to Barry Lomas that editorial control rested solely with the author and that he would give no-one (including the Pairc Trust) carte blanche on the script's content. This was to ensure the independence of the text and that contributions to the book would not contain any injurious or harmful comments to individuals or organisations.

Barry Lomas responded, declining to participate. This therefore led to no input from the previous landowner into the study and meant that the author was unable to take any of his views into consideration in the analysis and conclusions of the history of the community buyout.

The text also attempts to highlight the lessons that can be learnt from the Pairc Estate buyout for a number of organisations (and crofting communities) which may be involved in other community buyouts, including the Scottish Government. Indeed, some changes to land reform legislation which reflect the Pairc experience have already been approved by the Scottish Parliament.

It is, of course, for each reader to judge to what extent the author's aims have been achieved.

The Pairc Estate

CHARACTERISTICS OF THE ESTATE

The Pairc Estate is situated in the large parish of Lochs in south-east Lewis in the Outer Hebrides, off the north-west coast of Scotland. It is contained between two large sea lochs – Loch Erisort to the north and Loch Shell to the south. One long, easterly stretching arm of the head of Loch Seaforth forms part of the inland southern boundary of the estate. The eastern boundary of the estate comprises a long length of rocky, indented coastline. The long indentation formed by the sea loch of Loch Odhairn is a feature of the estate's eastern shoreline.

The estate first came into being as a separate land ownership unit in 1924 when Lord Leverhulme abandoned his plans for development in Lewis and sold off most of the island piecemeal as a number of separate private estates. Ownership of Pairc was transferred at that date from the Lewis and Harris Welfare and Development Company Ltd (one of Lord Leverhulme's companies) to Parc Crofters Ltd (later re-named Pairc Crofters Ltd) for the sum of £500. It is understood that Parc or Pairc Crofters Ltd (PCL) has been under the control of the Lomas family (or their relatives) since 1924, latterly Barry Lomas of Leamington Spa in Warwickshire in England though the family has retained a house in Harris from the early days of owning the Pairc Estate and continues to do so at the time of writing.

Unlike some of the other estates sold by Lord Leverhulme at this time (including the neighbouring Eishken and Soval Estates), there was no 'big house' or shooting lodge on Pairc, nor any 'in hand' land which the landlord could cultivate. As a result, the owners have never lived on the estate. The fishing rights were sold to Eishken and in more recent times the shooting rights have been leased to Soval. Virtually all the land is under crofting tenure in eleven crofting townships, each with separately tenanted crofts on the in bye land plus extensive common grazings over which the relevant crofters have various rights, including grazings rights for their livestock. The two major exceptions are land near and to the north of the abandoned settlement of Steimreway, which is subject to agricultural leases and land at Glen Gravir (see below).

Since 1924, significant parts of the original Pairc Estate have been sold. Up until December 2015 there were 261 sales of land on the estate. The most significant of these include Eilean Chaluim Chille (an island at the mouth of Loch Erisort) and part of the adjacent mainland of Lewis near Cromore which now forms the Crobeg Estate. There is also an area of some sixty acres at Glen Gravir now owned by the Scottish Government which was acquired by feu from Pairc Crofters Limited by the Department of Agriculture for Scotland in 1932 to create fifteen fishermen – cottar holdings for fishermen and squatters. Most of the other sales have been relatively small pieces of land which have been sold over the years, including for owner occupied crofts and areas feued off as sites for schools and service providers, or as house sites (a process which continues today).

The area bought in December 2015 by the community of Pairc was some 28,500 acres (11,540 hectares) – according to information supplied by Registers of Scotland. This comprised the great majority of the land which formed the Pairc Estate under the ownership of PCL immediately prior to the sale, apart from two parcels of land which were excluded from the sale. The first is a sizeable chunk of 435 acres (175 hectares) in the south-west corner of the estate adjoining the Eishken Estate, quite close to Eishken Lodge which the owner of Eishken wishes to purchase from PCL in order to safeguard the view from the lodge. At the time of writing this transaction has not taken place. The second is a small area of land of approximately 52 acres (21 hectares) just off the Gravir to Lemreway road south of Gravir. This was intended as the site of a converter station if the proposed inter connecter cable from Lewis to the mainland electricity grid was to leave the island at Gravir. However, it is unlikely that this land will now be used for this purpose because a preferred alternative has been identified at Arnish near Stornoway. The Pairc Trust has a right to purchase this site from PCL in certain circumstances after ten years if not used for the converter station.

A number of islands were included in the community's purchase. It is also worth noting that the foreshore between high and low water was eventually included in the buyout – a potentially important community economic asset.

The eleven crofting townships on the estate – Calbost, Caversta and Torasta, Cromore, Garyvard, Gravir, Habost, Kershader, Lemreway, Marvig, Orinsay, and Seaforth Head and Shildinish – contain some 214 crofts and around 400 people (not all of whom are crofters). The main area not subject to crofting tenure (apart from the foreshore) is the 3,500 acres (1,416 hectares) of the Steimreway grazings, subject to agricultural leases, in the south-west corner of the estate.

The land on the estate is predominantly comprised of upland moorland with a very large number of freshwater lochs and water courses. Apart from the in bye land close to the villages, which was traditionally cultivated for crops, the area is used extensively by crofters for grazing sheep and cattle. Sheep numbers today far outweigh those of cattle – a reversal of the situation before the twentieth century.

Numerous adjectives can be (and have been) used to describe the visual appearance of the area. A by no means exhaustive list would include the following terms, some of which complement one another and others of which represent conflicting views of the area: rugged, remote, austere, bleak, wild, empty, dramatic, attractive and beautiful.

ECONOMIC AND SOCIAL CHALLENGES

The number of active crofters and the amount of land actively crofted in Pairc, as elsewhere in the Outer Hebrides, have both declined for many years – a commonplace situation throughout the crofting areas of the Highlands and Islands. This, in the author's opinion, is a worrying trend because Lewis and the rest of the Outer Hebrides contain a large proportion of the total number of crofts and a huge area of common grazings. The islands also form the heartland of Scotland's Gaelic speaking communities and Gaelic culture.

Population decline on a large scale has characterised the Pairc area for over 100 years. For example, during the last century (the twentieth century) the population total of the Lochs parish area more than halved between 1901 and 2001, falling dramatically by 62 per cent from 4,733 to 1,814. This was the steepest decline of any Western Isles parish except Uig on the west side of Lewis. It is estimated that the population of what is now the Pairc Estate declined from some 1,800 to around 400 over the same period, an even steeper decline (78 per cent).

The main cause of the population loss has been the continuous out migration, especially of younger people, due to limited economic and social opportunities. This has resulted in not just far fewer people in the area but a heavily unbalanced and increasingly elderly population structure.

Whilst the main problems facing Pairc are similar to those confronting the rest of the Outer Hebrides – especially deprivation, social isolation, low incomes, limited employment opportunities, lack of facilities and resources, fuel poverty and a declining population – they are exacerbated in Pairc due to its particularly remote location. However, there are signs that the rate of population decline has eased in recent years with the movement of new families into the area.

An important characteristic of Pairc, and part of its identity and distinctiveness, is that it is an area where Gaelic is still widely spoken by a significant number of people on a daily basis. Over half of the population of the locality can speak the language and it has one of the highest proportions of Gaelic speakers and learners in Scotland. For many of its residents Gaelic remains an important and integral part of their life along with its associated customs and traditions – even though the traditional society of the area has, today, changed out of all recognition to what it was one or two generations ago.

HISTORY OF PAIRC

Much has been written about the history of the Pairc Estate and the wider Pairc area (which includes what is now the Eishken Estate) – particularly considering the relatively small geographical and population size of the area. This is due in large measure to the voluntary activity of the Pairc Historical Society – Comunn Eachdraidh na Pairc (the local historical society for the Pairc/South

Lochs area of Lewis). It has done sterling work in producing a wide variety of publications about the area over a considerable number of years. It also has a physical presence in the area in the form of an accredited museum at the Ravenspoint Centre at Kershader (which itself is a community-owned enterprise comprising a shop, fuel pumps, cafe, hostel and exhibition area). Credit should also go to The Islands Book Trust (previously based at Ravenspoint and now close by at Balallan) for its publishing outputs and events (conferences, talks, guided walks etc in and on the area), sometimes in collaboration with the Pairc Historical Society.

The aim of this chapter is not to attempt to present a comprehensive history of Pairc. Any readers with an interest in its history are referred to the publications listed in the bibliography. Instead, the purpose is to mention some of the more important historical events and characteristics of the area which will provide a relevant context for the buyout and help the reader's understanding and appreciation of the background to the purchase.

Two terms – 'Pairc' and 'South Lochs' – are in common usage in terminology and signage today in the Pairc Estate area. Many people take 'South Lochs' to mean the area occupied by the inhabited villages (these being the eleven crofting townships and their extensive common grazings) stretching from Seaforth Head and Shildinish in the west to Cromore, Marvig and Calbost in the east, and Gravir, Orinsay and Lemreway in the south. Therefore, the term 'South Lochs' can be viewed as being more or less synonymous with the Pairc Estate.

'Pairc' is an older term and one which was generally applied to the whole of the 'peninsula' – (including what is now the Eishken Estate) bounded on the north by Loch Erisort and on the west by the long Loch Seaforth – thus making 'Pairc' a much larger area than South Lochs or the Pairc Estate.

The term 'South Lochs' probably only came into relatively common usage after roads replaced boats as the main means of communication in and out of the 'peninsula' less than 100 years ago – thus better connecting it to the rest of Lewis, but simultaneously tending to reduce the links with some other parts of Lochs parish. Only a narrow neck of land (approximately one-and-a-half miles wide at its narrowest point) between the heads of Loch Erisort and

Loch Seaforth has prevented 'Pairc' from becoming an island in its own right. This has led to the apt description of 'Pairc' being 'almost an island within an island'.

This phrase 'almost an island within an island' symbolises the relative remoteness of the area even today, although there is now a much improved road network, enabling easier and quicker vehicle journey times and bringing Stornoway (with some 8,000 people, the only sizeable town in the Outer Hebrides) within daily commuting distance. However, considerable lengths of the road network on the estate remain single track with passing places and tortuous alignments (due to topography and the presence of the numerous freshwater lochs) – especially for settlements east and south of Garyvard. Orinsay and Lemreway, the two townships on the estate furthest away by road, are about a 60-miles round journey from Stornoway.

There is evidence of continuous human occupation of parts of the area for well over a thousand years. Many of the place and topographical names are of Norse origin, from the ninth century onwards – subsequently Gaelicised and Anglicised.

In more modern times, possibly from the fourteenth century and certainly from the seventeenth century, much of Pairc became a private deer park for the landowners of Lewis. People were likely to have been discouraged or even banned from living in large parts of it, prior to the development of the kelp and fishing industries in the second half of the eighteenth century when small coastal settlements were established in the former deer-hunting part of Pairc.

During the nineteenth century, large parts of Pairc were subject to the infamous Clearances following the establishment of the Pairc Sheep Farm in the early decades of the nineteenth century. The result was that all of the smaller settlements in the southern part of Pairc (south of Loch Shell) and several of the larger settlements on the northern shore of Loch Shell (on the present day Pairc Estate) – including Steimreway, Orinsay and Lemreway – were depopulated. Large numbers emigrated to Canada and North America, or moved to the Scottish mainland (particularly to the large cities) or other parts of Lewis. However, significant numbers remained in the area, many moving into the already congested coastal villages in the northern part of the Pairc estate – Habost, Kershader, Garyvard,

Cromore, Marvig, Calbost and Gravir (which were not cleared) – causing further severe overcrowding and insanitary conditions. Lemreway was resettled in 1857 when Steimreway was cleared and also became highly congested. Orinsay and Steimreway were re-occupied (the latter only temporarily for about 20 years between the early 1920s and the early 1940s) in the twentieth century following land raids in the 1920s.

CHAPTER ONE: SUMMARY AND REFLECTIONS

The Pairc Estate of some 28,500 acres forms part of the wider Pairc area which is one of the most remote and sparsely populated areas of Scotland. The land over this huge area is predominantly infertile upland moorland, with numerous freshwater lochs and a rugged coastline. For most of its history, sea transport was the main if not only realistic means of access to the outside world. There have been dramatic and often traumatic population changes over the years, with the clearance of some settlements in the nineteenth century coinciding with acute overcrowding and poverty in other villages, followed by a period of unrelenting rural depopulation during most of the twentieth century. Today the population is only around 400 people compared with nearly four times this level at the time of World War One.

The economic challenges facing the eleven small crofting townships of Pairc today, despite recent initiatives and some immigration from outside the area over the last few decades, continue to be severe. These problems, together with family memories of past hardships and perceived injustices, form the background to an understanding of why the Pairc community decided in the early twenty-first century that it wished to take ownership of its local estate in an attempt to build a better future.

First Steps

PROPOSAL FOR A COMMERCIAL WIND FARM IN PAIRC

The origins of the Pairc Estate community buyout can be traced to a meeting convened in Gravir in December 2002 attended by most (nine out of the eleven) local common grazings committee clerks and a number (six) of Pairc community councillors. The purpose of the meeting was to hear details of a possible large wind farm on part of the Pairc Estate proposed by the developer Scottish and Southern Energy (SSE) and Pairc Crofters Ltd (PCL), the company controlled by Barry Lomas which had formal ownership of the Pairc Estate.

The meeting was chaired by the late Donald Mackay, local councillor and previous convenor of Comhairle nan Eilean Siar (the local authority for the Western Isles). Ken Roddy Mackay, development officer of the Erisort Trust, a development body established in 2001 to benefit the local communities of Pairc and Kinloch, was also in attendance. Both Donald Mackay and Ken Roddy Mackay had some prior confidential knowledge of the wind farm proposal. Amongst the local common grazings committee representatives was Angus McDowall, the current and longstanding chairman of the Pairc Trust. He was representing the Habost common grazings committee.

The owners of the estate were represented by their factor, the late Simon Fraser – a highly respected Stornoway-based solicitor with considerable knowledge and experience of a wide range of crofting matters and legislation, and a very influential figure in several previous (and subsequent) community buyouts in the Highlands and Islands. Due to bad weather and travel problems the SSE representative (Alasdair MacSween who originally hails from Aignish near Stornoway) was unable to travel from the mainland. Simon Fraser therefore summarised the current position with the wind farm proposal.

It emerged that PCL and SSE had been in confidential discussions since 2001 on the potential for developing a commercial wind farm on part of the estate. However, the wind farm proposal was still at an early stage in its design and planning. No formal deal or legal agreement had been reached between the two parties. Ken Roddy Mackay suggested that a local liaison group should be set up to meet SSE, to move the project forward and to give accurate information back to the community. Simon Fraser concurred, suggesting that the liaison group should consist of four or five representatives of the whole community. Its aim should be to lay the ground rules for the future, to make a case for as much benefit as possible from the wind farm development to be retained in the Pairc area, and to liaise with SSE and the community to ensure that the best possible consultation took place. It was agreed that six representatives from the meeting would meet with Alasdair MacSween from SSE the next day. Also, following this, a public meeting would be arranged as soon as possible in order for the wider community to be informed of the proposal and to be given an opportunity to discuss it.

The public meeting took place on 23 January 2003 at the Ravenspoint Centre, Kershader, chaired by Donald Mackay and attended by around fifty people. Alasdair MacSween of SSE indicated that the proposed wind farm could consist of 125 turbines each 180ft high (67m), and some 35 miles of access tracks. He said that around £250,000 from the developer could go into a community fund annually for twenty-five years over the lifetime of the wind farm, with an option for the development to continue beyond this initial period (subject to various consents) either in its original form or through replacement turbines and any necessary new or upgraded infrastructure. Alasdair MacSween also stated that a number of important surveys and studies were necessary and that it would be at least another year before it would be known whether or not the project was viable. In addition to the community fund, the landowner and relevant crofters would receive compensation under crofting legislation for land resumed for the development.

Resumption is the process of a landlord taking land out of crofting tenure – and therefore out of a crofting tenant's use – for some purpose of her/his own or that of a third party. Resumption of croft land has been regulated by statute since the Crofters Holdings (Scotland) Act 1886.

Other speakers at the meeting included Henk Munneke of HIE, and Ken Roddy Mackay of the Erisort Trust. The latter raised the need for a body such as a charitable trust to be established in order to ensure that the benefits remain within the community. There were various suggestions from the audience as to how the total amount of money available from the development could be apportioned between the community, the landowner and the crofters – for example, 60 per cent community, 20 per cent landowner, 20 per cent crofters; or 40 per cent community, 30 per cent landowner, 30 per cent crofters. However, the meeting agreed this was a matter that should be taken forward on the community's behalf by the liaison group that was to be formed at the meeting.

THE PAIRC COMMUNITY LIAISON GROUP

A liaison group – later known as the Pairc Community Liaison group (PCLG) – was formed at the meeting, the five members being local councillor Donald Mackay of Gravir; Donald John Macdonald of Kershader; Angus McDowall of Habost; and Morris Black and Steve Mortimore, both of Garyvard. Ken Roddy Mackay also joined the group in his Erisort Trust officer role in order to assist in its development. The group felt that it was important at that stage to have as wide a remit as possible, with the prime role of progressing the initiative with the developer of the wind farm in the best interests of the local community.

It should be noted that there was from the start some ambiguity in the use of terms such as 'taking forward' or 'progressing' the wind farm development proposal – it is not clear whether this assumed that the development was going to or should proceed, or whether it was open to the liaison group to oppose the development if that was the view of the community. Even at this early stage there was a feeling amongst some members of the community who did not favour a wind farm that the membership of the liaison group had been arranged in advance so that there was a pro-wind farm majority, despite members having been formally elected at the meeting.

It is evident from the first meeting note produced by the group in late January 2003 that its members were well attuned to the complexity and range of issues that they needed to consider. The overall impression was of the group's astuteness, realism, determination and ambition. Even at this early stage of the process the group was aware of the need to establish a more formal trust with a written constitution as a mechanism for moving matters forward and in order to be able to access funds and submit various funding (and other) applications.

The group also acknowledged that the work being carried out by Ken Roddy Mackay, and other expenses incurred by the Erisort Trust, needed to be paid for; and that without this input the liaison group would be unable to operate. SSE agreed to make a sum of money available to enable part of Ken Roddy Mackay's time to be paid for to help develop the wind farm project at a local level and to act as a liaison point between the community, the developer and the estate. It is worth mentioning, for the record, that two members of the liaison group (Angus McDowall and Donald John Macdonald) were also directors of the Erisort Trust.

Throughout January, February and March 2003 the liaison group met frequently, discussing a wide range of topics. Members of the liaison group met with local crofters and participated in a visit (accompanied by Barry Lomas and Simon Fraser) to an existing wind farm near Campbeltown in Argyllshire. The liaison group met with Barry Lomas on 3 April 2003. This appears to be the first time that the group raised with him an alternative approach involving a community buyout of the estate, which had been discussed in their first meeting with local crofters. The first approach was that outlined by Alasdair MacSween at the January 2003 public meeting – that is, of the estate remaining in the ownership of PCL but the local community benefitting from a substantial annual community fund derived from the wind farm's profit. The second approach of a community buyout may have been triggered by recent legislation, the Land Reform (Scotland) Act 2003, passed by the Scottish Parliament which under Part 3 gave crofting communities the opportunity to buy crofting land even against the wishes of the landlord if they could persuade Scottish Ministers that this was in the public interest and could meet the other requirements of the Act. A community buyout could also come about through a voluntary transfer of ownership of the estate to the local community if the landlord agreed to sell – as has happened in a number of other areas since the purchase of the North Lochinver Estate by Assynt crofters in 1992.

Barry Lomas's initial reaction to the second approach, of a community buyout, seems to have been that the estate was not presently for sale although this might change in the future. The liaison group believed at that stage that, if the community was to attempt to buy the estate, a voluntary transfer (a so-called 'amicable' transfer) was preferable compared with the use of Part 3 of the Act (a so-called 'hostile' bid). Barry Lomas made it clear that he was opposed to a 'hostile' bid. He appeared to want to work with the community in order not to frighten off the wind farm developer. This seems to have been an acknowledgement by the landlord of the importance of local community support so that the developer would have confidence in investing substantial sums of money early on in the process in order to secure the necessary consents to construct and run the wind farm. When pressed by the liaison group about a possible community buyout, according to the group's meeting notes Barry Lomas confirmed that he was not opposed to a buyout in principle. The author has assumed that he was referring to the possibility of a voluntary transfer of the estate rather than a forced purchase under Part 3 of the Land Reform Act.

It seems apparent from this meeting that frustration was beginning to escalate on both sides – Barry Lomas representing PCL on the one hand and the liaison group representing the local community on the other. The liaison group appeared unable to move things along quickly enough in the direction that Barry Lomas wished – in order to secure a deal with the developer with the support of the local community to the wind farm proposal. On the other hand, he seemed according to the liaison group to be skating around things instead of giving clear answers. For example, his attitude towards a community purchase of the estate appeared ambivalent – while opposed to a 'hostile buyout', he seemed willing to consider an 'amicable transfer', but not at present.

The liaison group decided to arrange a public meeting on 16 April to ascertain the feeling of the community as a whole towards the proposed wind farm. Forty-eight residents attended, with Donald John Macdonald in the chair in Donald Mackay's absence. He gave a presentation covering the SSE proposal, the alternative of a community buyout, and the landowner's reactions to points put to him by the liaison group. He set out a number of more detailed options available to the community, based on the two broad approaches and stated that a vote would take place on them at the end of the meeting. When the meeting was opened to questions Donald John Macdonald replied 'no' when asked if the landlord was amenable to a buyout. To the question 'what does the lease agreement say or do', he replied 'we do not know ... we believe the lease agreement has still to be signed'. It should be noted that there was understandable confusion at this time about exactly what legal undertakings had been entered into by PCL and SSE regarding a wind farm – see chapters three and four for clarification on the initial Option Agreement, and the later interposed lease and sub-lease (details of which were not available to the liaison group).

The meeting then moved on to vote on five options put to it. These were:

- Option 1 Accept the current offer (this was presumably the proposal put forward by SSE at the meeting on 23 January) – this received 0 votes
- Option 2 Negotiate an improved offer – this received 34 votes
- Option 3 Buy into the project (meaning the community owning part of the project, for example a certain number of turbines) – this received 6 votes
- Option 4 Buy the estate (presumably this could be either under Part 3 of the Land Reform Act or a voluntary transfer) – this received 31 votes
- Option 5 Reject the development – this received 0 votes

Following the vote, those present were asked if they were content for the liaison group to act on behalf of the community to take matters forward with the developer and landowner. This was agreed by an overwhelming show of hands.

The liaison group was very much aware of the need for professional assistance on several fronts in order to move forward a number of important matters, particularly the two options most favoured by the public meeting. For example, one essential task was to arrange for an independent valuation to be undertaken of the estate in order to estimate its market value in the event of a buyout. Another involved financial and taxation issues, particularly for crofters, advice on which was sought from the accountant Allan MacAskill of Commercial and Industrial Business Services (CIB) in Stornoway. HIE, mainly through its Community Land Unit (CLU), would also have a critical advisory role to play throughout the process, as subsequent events were to demonstrate.

At a political level, Donald Mackay stood down as a local councillor in 2003 although he remained chairman of the liaison group. He was succeeded as the local councillor on CnES by Annie Macdonald. The liaison group wished to gain her involvement and support for taking the two options forward. The local MSP Alasdair Morrison also expressed a keen interest in helping the liaison group in any way he could. Calling in the expertise of a variety of individuals and organisations was seen by the liaison group as not only essential for taking matters forward; but also as a means for community engagement and dissemination of information to people in the area in order to retain and strengthen support for the liaison group's work.

In July 2003, Allan MacAskill produced a short discussion document for the liaison group, which included an option which assumed the community would take ownership of the estate with the agreement of the landlord. This was based on the principle that PCL should be compensated for foregoing ownership of the estate and the potential accruing benefits – although the purchase price of the estate and the scope, nature, mechanics and value of such compensation were yet to be determined. For example, his document suggested that, if the estate was transferred to the community at no cost and there was a total estimated annual income of £876,000 available for allocation from the wind farm after the development company had taken its share, a 20 per cent share of this allocation for PCL would result in it receiving £3.5 million over a twenty year period, and the community receiving £14.0 million over the same period. If the purchase price for the estate was £200,000, the total sum received by PCL from the wind farm would be adjusted downwards by this amount. Other time periods (5, 10 and 15 years) and shares for PCL (5 per cent, 10, 15, 25, 30 and 33 per cent) were also set out in Allan MacAskill's document.

This was used by the liaison group as the basis for discussion at a meeting with local common grazings clerks in the middle of July. At that meeting the liaison group recapped on the possible

financial arrangements if the wind farm was constructed. It
presented various ways in which the revenue from the wind farm
could be split between PCL and the local community if a voluntary
community buyout took place. It seems that the view of crofters
was hardening that the maximum the community should accept as
PCL's share of the total estimated annual income from the wind farm
available for allocation should be 20 per cent. The alternative of a
'hostile' buyout was emphasised by Donald Mackay in the event of
insufficient progress being made with PCL.

So, by summer 2003 it was becoming clear that there were actually
three strategic options available to the Pairc community:

(a) The estate remaining in private ownership. In the event of
a wind farm development the community could negotiate
with the developer to establish a community fund of a size
acceptable to the local community. While there was no legal
obligation on a developer to establish one, it was accepted
practice and a community fund could be made a condition
of a consent for a commercial wind farm.

(b) A negotiated voluntary purchase of the estate. This was
dependent on the willingness of the owner to sell. If the
landlord was willing to sell, the purchase price would
depend on negotiations between the community and the
owner along the lines of the options in Allan MacAskill's
paper.

(c) A so-called 'hostile' buyout of the estate. Under Part 3 of
the new legislation, the community would need to
demonstrate to Scottish Ministers that the procedures of
the Act had been followed and that it was in the overall
public interest for the land to change hands. The purchase
price would be based on an independent valuation – which
would take into account the prospects for a wind farm at
the time of valuation. Of course, Part 3 of the Act had never
been used before so this was unknown territory.

The liaison group met with representatives of SSE on 25 July 2003.
It blamed the landowner for the lack of progress – which was also
causing concern for SSE. The group emphasised its mandate from
the community and outlined the options available to the community
– a voluntary or a hostile buyout, or the option of negotiating
a high level of community benefit with the estate remaining in

private ownership. Alasdair MacSween from SSE suggested that without flexibility on the issue of the proportion of the potential revenue stream for PCL being increased there was little point in the community representatives having a further meeting with the landowner.

However, the liaison group (and SSE) did meet with Barry Lomas, in fact shortly afterwards on the same day. At that meeting Donald Mackay reviewed events to date including the mandate to purchase the estate. He expressed a desire to talk only about general principles but wondered what compensation would meet the landlord's aspirations. No figure seems to have been mentioned in response. However, according to the liaison group's record of the meeting, Barry Lomas confirmed that he would forego ownership of the estate as long as he was sufficiently compensated. Alasdair MacSween asked about possible revenue streams and made it clear that SSE was very anxious to get a move on. It was explained that the liaison group planned to have meetings the following week to sort out the figures and then meet with the landowner, hopefully to agree terms.

A further meeting took place on 7 August on a one-to-one basis between Barry Lomas and Allan MacAskill who represented the liaison group. He asked whether or not Barry Lomas had considered the group's view on the maximum share (20 per cent) which it felt the community would accept as PCL's share of the income from the wind farm. According to a note of the meeting, Barry Lomas responded that he had indicated in March that he had advised the liaison group verbally, that he was willing to accept somewhere between 34 and 38 per cent and would not commit to any further offer or movement below this range. However, the note indicates that he stressed that he wished to continue discussions. And also that he felt that legal formalities and other matters could proceed without there being a conclusion to the financial discussions. Allan MacAskill said that his understanding was that the liaison group was not prepared to go to a public meeting with any proposal in excess of 20 per cent for PCL's share of total annual income. Negotiations for a voluntary transfer of the estate therefore stalled. The main emphasis of the liaison group's considerations was therefore at that point switching to the possibility of a community buyout under Part 3 of the Land Reform Act.

By now the prospect of a large wind farm was also evidently dividing opinion amongst the local community. Not everyone welcomed such a proposal. Anecdotally it appears that opposition was strongest amongst more recent incomers to the area rather than longstanding residents, although this was by no means a clear cut division. Events came to a head at the end of August 2003 when some thirty people (including children) held a noisy demonstration outside Ken Roddy Mackay's office in Kershader prior to a meeting of the liaison group which Barry Lomas was attending. The protesters were members of the Pairc Protection Group (PPG) – a group that had been formed to oppose the wind farm proposal. The protesters claimed that the liaison group was not representative of the community and had no community mandate and was not consulting with it. PPG handed in a letter for the liaison group setting out its concerns, but by this time Donald Mackay (who was to chair the meeting) had called the police. When the police arrived they were told that the protesters were not local people, although it seems that most of them did live in Pairc even though some were recent incomers to the area.

At the meeting the liaison group passed a vote of no confidence in one of its members. This was apparently in the (disputed and unsubstantiated) belief that he had been leaking information to his partner, an active member of the PPG. At a subsequent public meeting, a new liaison group was formally established omitting the member in question, although there was little discussion of this proposal which it seems likely had been arranged by the other members of the liaison group in advance. The liaison group had decided that from now on its chair would be the sole contact with the landowner in order to better maintain confidentiality. The decision to remove one of its members certainly did nothing to heal the divisions in the community over the wind farm. It is also likely to have had an adverse impact on the productivity of the liaison group, reducing its membership to four (plus support from Ken Roddy Mackay).

MOVES TO SET UP A NEW COMMUNITY BODY

The liaison group convened an evening public meeting at Gravir School for 16 September 2003 to consider the next steps. This was well attended. A number of speakers had been arranged for the meeting: Sandra Holmes of HIE's Community Land Unit; Henk Munneke from HIE; Kenneth MacLeod – solicitor for the liaison group; John Campbell QC – who it was hoped could provide specialist legal advice to the liaison group; and Annie Macdonald the local CnES councillor.

The meeting focussed on what steps needed to be taken to proceed with a community buyout of the estate. An important item for discussion was the setting up of a new community organisation which would serve as the vehicle through which the Pairc community could become owners of the Pairc Estate if an application were to be made for Scottish Ministers' consent to purchase the estate under Part 3 of the Land Reform Act. The Act sets out detailed requirements in relation to crofting community buyouts, including provisions in relation to the constitution of the buyout organisation. This had to take the form of a company limited by guarantee incorporating the legislative requirements in its constitution (its Memorandum and Articles of Association). Only a company so constituted would qualify for HIE and Scottish Land Fund financial assistance to acquire assets. PCLG, as an ad hoc group, would not have met the requirements to acquire assets, though both HIE and the SLF could have provided assistance to it if necessary to help develop a buyout proposal if PCLG had chosen to go down that route. In the end, HIE provided some financial support to the Erisort Trust to help advance the buyout plans because it was considered to be a more appropriate body than PCLG as it was incorporated and had a bank account and operational experience. The Memorandum and Articles dealt with the role, remit and powers of the company and its administration; membership (a company limited by guarantee does not have shareholders); election of directors; and the conduct of meetings of members and directors.

A draft of the Memorandum and Articles (drawn up by the liaison group's solicitor, Kenneth MacLeod) of a new community organisation (which would become the Pairc Trust) was presented to the meeting. This attracted much discussion. Copies were also made available for consultation at local post offices, the Erisort Trust office and electronically from HIE. Once, and provided that the community ratified the document the new company could be formed. The next steps would be to establish the membership (detailed in the draft) and to hold an inaugural AGM to elect its first directors.

Sandra Holmes explained that the forming of a new company did not by itself place any obligation on the community to proceed with the purchase of the estate. However, a properly constituted community body was necessary in order to pursue a community buyout under the Land Reform (Scotland) Act 2003. Moreover, before such an application could be made under Part 3 of the Act, it would be necessary to follow certain procedures, including the holding of a ballot to determine whether a community buyout had the support of the community. She emphasised that the buyout was in no way dependent on the proposed wind farm; and also that a feasibility study (by independent consultants and funded by HIE and SLF) would be useful to consider the economic, social and environmental potential of the estate's assets and the viability of various development opportunities. Whilst a wind farm proposal could provide considerable income opportunities for the local community, there was no guarantee that a large scale wind farm would be developed and therefore she recommended that the community should ascertain the viability of community ownership of the estate in the absence of a wind farm.

Prior to the meeting, five motions (three emanating from one person) had been presented to the liaison group for consideration at it. These related to the timescale and procedures for establishing a new trust (in the form of a company limited by guarantee). It is not clear why this was done though it may have reflected some disquiet in parts of the community with the way in which matters were being handled and taken forward. One motion, for example, called for a secret ballot of the entire community as to whether or not it should accept the setting up of a trust and its proposed Memorandum and Articles. However, on an overwhelming show of hands, the meeting approved a motion endorsing the continuance of the liaison group until such time as a trust was established and directors appointed. Another public meeting of 9 October agreed the Memorandum and Articles and the issue of membership forms for the new company.

Meanwhile, the liaison group had met with Barry Lomas on 23 September and expressed dissatisfaction with the amount of progress made. It felt that an impasse had been reached and that this had to be addressed. A week later the liaison group met with the local authority CnES which agreed to give its full support in helping with negotiations and also pledged to give financial assistance towards a buyout.

In October 2003 the liaison group (via the Erisort Trust) requested a valuation (which was funded by HIE) from the District Valuer of the Pairc Estate for community buyout purposes. An interim valuation and report was issued by the District Valuer within one week, on the basis that the landowner would supply further information with regard to rental income and also provide sight of all leases which were in effect on the estate in order to allow him to issue a more definitive valuation. However, by July 2004 that information had not been forthcoming so the District Valuer issued his final report that month without it. In that report the District Valuer stated:

I am surprised the landowner cannot or will not furnish you with the required information; it is in their interest so to do. That being said it would appear that, in valuation terms, there is nothing 'hidden' or new which would give rise to a material alteration to my valuation. However, if all the relevant information had been provided I would not need to caveat my valuation in terms as I do at the current date i.e. the valuation would carry a definitive weight not currently available.

The District Valuer's opinion in July 2004 (subject to various assumptions and caveats etc) was that the market value of the Pairc Estate ignoring an element of hope value pertinent to wind farm generation was £110,000. And that the market value with hope value was £120,000 – a difference between the two valuations of only £10,000.

His assessment of the wind farm proposal is of considerable interest:

I am asked also to comment upon an element of hope value, which may arise, over the base market value, in connection with a wind farm proposal for a 250MW wind farm. It is considered unlikely that a development on this scale will be pursued and there are major negative factors which have to be borne in mind when considering this issue. The primary factor which a potential purchaser would have to take into account is the upgrading of the main grid connection. Without this connection I cannot see a 250 MW wind farm ever being constructed. Any element of hope value at the current date would, in my opinion, be nominal only. I am of the view that a purchaser would view this prospect as too risky and an overbid but [sic] give rise to future disposal difficulties if the scheme did not come to fruition.

Clearly, the value of the land will have an element of hope value (this is true of every land sale) but the difficulty here is identifying that part which can be attributed to the wind farm potential. The sums of money involved for wind farm schemes are significant. It is expected that a 250MW scheme could realise significant rental income flowing to the landlord. However attractive this appears on paper it must, in my view, be seen as highly speculative and not realistic. There are too many imponderables to make a realistic judgement in terms of effect upon market value. At current date the inter connector cable required to transmit wind farm electricity generated on Lewis is not laid nor is there any timetable for so doing; there are difficulties on the mainland with regard to proposals for the new improved overhead line from Beauly to Denny; there is no overhead line whatsoever from Ullapool (where the inter connector would landfall) to Beauly and there is a growing tide of opposition on the islands themselves against wind farm generation. All of these factors suggest to me that a prospective purchaser would be ill advised to bid up on the potential income which might flow from a wind farm being situated on Pairc Estate.

I am aware of the option agreement signed between the landlord and Scottish and Southern Energy and it is noted that a payment of £5,000 was made to the landlord. It could be argued this should be seen as current hope value. In addition I have some limited market evidence to support hope value at or around this level attributable to wind farm potential The more likely scenario is a smaller scale development which a purchaser can readily see demand for without taking a huge risk in terms of a 250 MW development.

If a smaller scale development is proposed a rent in the order of £50,000 might be achievable. This would not translate into market value at current date as it would require deferment until such time as a scheme came on stream. I understand that the lead in time for any scheme is likely to be in the order of 5 – 10 years. I would consider any element of hope value to be relatively small at current date given the circumstances pertaining at present. That is not to say that the hope value element would always stay low – if planning consent was granted, the grid connection secured etc then the hope value element would likely rise.

I remain of the view that for the present moment a purchaser would be unwise to overbid on an issue which clearly has some way to go before any wind farm income generation could reasonably be anticipated.

By late October 2003 the liaison group had still not altogether abandoned hope of coming to an agreement with the landlord for a voluntary transfer. A meeting was held on 1 December 2003 between the PCLG, PCL and SSE facilitated by CnES. SSE referred to an Option and Lease Agreement with PCL and expressed concern that this had not yet been signed and wished to have a signed agreement with Barry Lomas by the following week. Alasdair MacSween (SSE) told the meeting that his company wished to take the community and crofters forward with them and that the Option and Lease Agreement contained nothing to prejudice their interests. However, PCLG expressed concern that whilst PCL and SSE had had eighteen months in which to prepare an agreement, the liaison group had only seen the document for the first time the previous week. The liaison group had concerns about the document and stated its primary focus was now the transfer of landownership to which Barry Lomas responded that the estate was not for sale.

SSE did not see the points raised by the liaison group as jeopardising the legal agreement which would be between the developer (SSE) and the landowner (PCL). In reply, the liaison group requested a formal response to its concerns from SSE and asked for an Ancillary Agreement with it which would take account of crofters' interests, allay their fears and galvanise community support. The liaison group felt that an Ancillary Agreement needed to be finalised prior to the legal agreement between SSE and PCL. It wanted a legally binding agreement with both landowner and developer so that there could be no back tracking or changing of minds later on.

CHAPTER TWO: SUMMARY AND REFLECTIONS

This chapter has covered the initial stages of the story of the Pairc community buyout during the year prior to the formal establishment of the Pairc Trust at the end of 2003. During this time, the Pairc community's dealings with landlord Barry Lomas and his involvement with emerging plans for a commercial wind farm on the estate in conjunction with SSE were handled by an 'ad hoc' Pairc Community Liaison Group (PCLG) initially formed to represent the community without a written constitution in late 2002.

It is clear that the trigger for the formation of the liaison group was the prospect of a large wind farm on the Pairc Estate rather than a strong desire from the outset for the community to buy the estate. The proposal for a wind farm was put forward by Barry Lomas and his commercial partners, not by anyone in the Pairc community. Initial discussions with the community representatives centred on how projected income from the planned development might be split between the landlord, local crofters, and others in the Pairc community. Only somewhat later did the idea of a community buyout of the estate, whether through a voluntary ('amicable') or Part 3 ('hostile') approach, emerge as options for the community in reacting to the wind farm proposal.

With the benefit of hindsight, it can be seen that these origins had a strong bearing on future tensions and problems which arose in relation to the arguments within the local community for or against a community land buyout. The liaison group was seen by some in the community as favouring or even promoting the wind farm, and the handling of the public demonstration and change in the composition of the liaison group reinforced this perception. In this were sown the seeds of later mistrust between some local people and the Pairc Trust or certain directors of the Trust.

Other future themes of the Pairc buyout can also perhaps be recognised in these early months. One was the mixed messages which appeared to be emanating from Barry Lomas, who at one meeting seemed to be saying that the estate was not for sale, and at another that he was not against a community purchase in principle. He was possibly referring to his opposition to a 'hostile' buyout but a willingness to consider a voluntary transfer, but this appears not to be clear. Another was the recognition that the local community needed professional advice on many aspects of the complex options which were rapidly opening up – particularly on legal, financial, and administrative aspects. It is to the credit of the liaison group that advice was sought and acted on relatively speedily – in particular, the moves taken to set up what became the Pairc Trust with a formal constitution consistent with the requirements of the newly passed Land Reform (Scotland) Act 2003 and as recommended by HIE and legal advisers.

Finally, it is clear that relations between Barry Lomas and the Pairc community representatives quickly deteriorated and became fragile from early on. There were repeated complaints from the community side about lack of progress and not being properly informed about the Option Agreement under discussion between Barry Lomas and SSE about the wind farm. There was a feeling in some quarters, rightly or wrongly, that the landlord was not genuinely interested in transferring ownership of the estate to the community and that he was putting and would continue to put obstacles in the way of this. On his side, Barry Lomas possibly saw the protests by the Pairc Protection Group as evidence of divisions within the local community. However, matters did not deteriorate into open confrontation until later, in 2004 and 2005. By this time the Pairc Trust had decided to submit an application under Part 3 of the Act for consent to purchase the estate compulsorily, and the existence of the landlord's interposed lease was revealed (see chapter four). A basic lack of trust between the two sides was clearly evident at this point.

CHAPTER THREE

The First Part 3 Application

The Pairc Trust was incorporated (and registered with Companies House) on 19 December 2003. An election for the first directors was held on 16 February 2004. Ten directors were elected from nineteen candidates – a healthy start for the Trust in terms of local interest in the new organisation. Voting was open to all members of the Trust, in accordance with the Trust's Memorandum and Articles. In short, voting membership was open to all those over the age of sixteen who were: (a) resident within the boundaries of the estate or (b) the tenant of a croft on the estate and resident within 16 kilometres.

The year 2004 proved to be an extremely busy one for the Trust. Although negotiations with the landowner continued in parallel on the possibility of a voluntary buyout, by the summer of that year much time was being devoted to preparing an application to Scottish Ministers for consent to purchase the estate under Part 3 of the Land Reform (Scotland) Act 2003.

Establishment of the Trust was a major early step towards the local community being able to achieve its ownership ambitions. The right to buy under the provisions of Part 3 of the Act could only be exercised by a properly constituted crofting community body (CCB). Setting up of the Pairc Trust, in the way it was done, fulfilled that requirement.

However, preparation of a right to buy application required considerable work and expense. The detailed procedures are set out in Part 3 of the Land Reform (Scotland) Act 2003 and its associated secondary legislation. Furthermore, no application for consent to purchase under Part 3 could succeed without the support in a ballot of both the crofting community as a whole (which included local residents who were not crofters) and those who were croft tenants of land located within the Pairc Estate area.

FEASIBILITY STUDY

In order to assist the community in assessing the benefits of community ownership (of either a negotiated purchase or a right to buy option) it was agreed that a feasibility study would be useful to identify the economic, social and environmental potential of the estate. Consultants Strutt and Parker in association with independent consultants Carola Bell and Agnes Rennie (both residents of Ness on the Isle of Lewis) and accountants Johnston Carmichael were commissioned by the Trust, in May 2004, to undertake the study to appraise the potential of the estate under community ownership. A key component was to address the viability of community ownership without the wind farm proposal – which was, therefore, excluded from it. Highlands and Islands Enterprise (HIE) funded the research and the consultants' report was completed in October 2004.

The landlord declined a request from the consultants for information regarding the estate's accounts. The consultants therefore constructed an assumed set of accounts based on the limited information available and their professional knowledge and expertise. Despite the estate having been run on a fairly inactive basis, Strutt and Parker estimated a modest annual surplus of £5,000 and considered the business to be stable and viable. They also concluded that under community ownership and with active management, the estate had the potential to become more sustainable and to deliver added community benefits, without the proposed wind farm.

The process of community involvement in the study was viewed by the Trust to be just as important as the final report and plan itself. It wished to see community liaison and ways of involving the community in generating and assessing development ideas for the estate as key components of the exercise. To that end, three public meetings were held; plus discussions with local businesses, a playgroup committee and youth group. These were led by Agnes Rennie and Carola Bell. In addition, a number of individuals contacted Strutt and Parker direct.

As a result, several development options were identified and examined by Strutt and Parker to investigate their potential. They then gave further consideration to the three development options with the greatest potential to add longer term viability to the estate's businesses. These were: (a) sporting – shooting and fishing leases; (b) housing – house sites for sale at both affordable and market rates, and rented social housing; and (c) tourism – comprising an island heritage centre with tearoom/restaurant, and caravan/camping.

The feasibility study was a significant step forward for both the Trust and the local community. It demonstrated convincingly that community ownership in the absence of a wind farm was viable and sustainable. However, it placed no obligation on the community to proceed with a buyout. That would be determined, in due course, by a formal ballot in accordance with Part 3 of the Land Reform (Scotland) Act 2003. A ballot was also a requirement of HIE and the Scottish Land Fund (SLF) with respect to funding applications for financial assistance in order to help buy the estate.

DECIDING THE WAY FORWARD

The Trust required legal advice on a number of fronts, particularly in relation to ongoing negotiations with PCL and SSE, and to progress its Part 3 application. Lindsays, a long established and experienced firm of Scottish lawyers, was commissioned to fulfil this role, with Roy Shearer (a partner in the firm based in Edinburgh) as the main contact. He became a key figure in the buyout story from April 2004 onwards.

The Trust first asked Roy Shearer to advise it on the Option Agreement between PCL and SSE, which had been signed on 19 December 2003 – coincidentally the same date as the Trust was incorporated. The purposes of the Option Agreement were firstly to enable SSE to carry out detailed investigations to establish whether or not a wind farm on the Pairc Estate would be viable; and secondly to ensure that the estate owner would be bound to grant SSE a lease on agreed terms so that it could develop a wind farm if one proved viable and planning permission could be obtained.

Without such an agreement, there could have been a risk to SSE that, after it had incurred the considerable expense of establishing the viability of a wind farm and obtaining planning permission, the owner would have been free to reach a deal with another wind farm developer. In such circumstances, a rival developer might have been prepared to offer more attractive terms than SSE, even though they had not incurred the preliminary expense to establish the wind farm's viability.

It should be noted that proceeding by way of an Option Agreement such as that entered into between PCL and SSE was normal practice at this early stage of a potential project. It provided greater assurance for SSE pending detailed site investigations, obtaining consent for the wind farm from Scottish Government, and getting agreement from the Scottish Land Court to the resumption of the necessary land. Although no formal lease of the land which would be required for the wind farm had been entered into, its terms had been agreed in draft by the two parties. It was expected that a lease in terms of the agreed draft would be put in place once the site investigations, planning permission and resumption were finalised.

As was standard practice, the Option Agreement had annexed to it a draft lease setting out the terms on which the parts of the estate needed to enable the wind farm development to go ahead would be leased to SSE. Those parts of the estate would have been identified during the planning process. The draft lease would have had to be amplified to identify those parts, but only when the actual lease was put in place, after the planning process.

The Option Agreement also included a draft of a Standard Security, the purpose of which was to prevent PCL avoiding its contractual liabilities under the Option Agreement by, for example, conveying the estate to a third party. That Standard Security was signed and registered in the Register of Sasines immediately following the signing of the Option Agreement. However, because of the way the 2003 Act was worded, it would not have been effective to avoid the estate passing to a third party, namely the Pairc Trust, if the Trust had purchased the estate using the powers in the Act.

The result would have been that, albeit unintentionally on the part of PCL, the contractual obligations in the Option Agreement, which would have required PCL to grant a lease in terms of the draft, would have become unenforceable. PCL had proceeded as normal in relation to a prospective wind farm development before it and/or SSE realised the possible consequences of the introduction of the crofting community right to buy.

As part of his detailed advice, Roy Shearer expressed the opinion that, if it bought the estate, the Trust would not be bound by the Option Agreement entered into between PCL and SSE. If so minded the local community, as owner of the estate, could (through the Trust) enter into an agreement with a different wind farm developer, ignoring the existing Option Agreement. Roy Shearer also highlighted the risk to PCL and SSE that the crofting community (due to the fact that the land needed for the wind farm was currently under crofting tenure and would have to be resumed, to which not all of the crofters might agree, and partly due to their ability to force PCL to sell the estate) might thereby negate the agreement which SSE had with PCL. Before a wind farm development could go ahead there would have to be separate negotiations with the crofters, who had the right to occupy the land which would be required for the wind farm, in relation to the compensation to which they would be entitled on resumption, which could be far from straightforward. In such a situation the risk was that SSE might decide that moving forward satisfactorily and quickly enough would be just too complicated and would therefore pull out altogether.

On the other hand, Roy Shearer advised that if the estate was a really attractive location for a wind farm then, even if SSE were to pull out, it might be perfectly possible to attract another developer – or even to renegotiate the deal with SSE. He concluded that the Trust was in a strong position as a result of the land being under crofting tenure and needing to be resumed and the fact that the crofters had not been involved by PCL and SSE in the negotiations which had resulted in the Option Agreement having been entered into.

Roy Shearer was also asked by the Trust to comment on the pros and cons of acquiring the estate through a voluntary sale compared with a Part 3 purchase. With the Trust now in place as a Crofting Community Body (CCB) in terms of the 2003 Act it was able to enter into more formal negotiations with the landowner. As things stood at the time, Roy Shearer did not consider that starting off on the voluntary route would in any way prevent the Trust reverting to the Part 3 route if the former appeared unlikely to deliver the desired results for the local community. He regarded the Part 3 route as being available to the Trust as a backup if negotiations broke down.

He felt that any disagreement with the landowner would likely be about money rather than anything else – with the landowner wanting to achieve as high a sale price as possible and the Trust wanting to pay as little as possible. Although the Trust had been advised (by the District Valuer) that the hope value associated with the wind farm proposal was small, Roy Shearer speculated that the landowner would be receiving contrary advice and that is why Barry Lomas, in his opinion, was probably doing all he could to advance the deal with SSE as quickly as possible so as to increase the likelihood of the wind farm development going ahead. Progress would, however, also be conditional on consent being granted by Scottish Ministers for the wind farm, and the SLC approving the resumption of the land involved. SSE no doubt also had its own agenda and timetable.

However, in the second half of 2004, the position changed fundamentally when two separate leases were put in place – in August between PCL and a new company which Barry Lomas had formed under the name of Pairc Renewables Ltd (PRL); and in November between PRL and SSE – see chapter four. It must have been decided that an Option Agreement and draft lease (which would have been backed up by a security granted by PCL to SSE to guarantee PCL's good faith) was a less satisfactory way of proceeding than the granting of a lease, which would give SSE a formal lease document which could be registered in the Land Register. With an actual lease in place, Roy Shearer felt that the position might be different. He did not rule out the possibility that going down the voluntary route could result in the Trust being bound by an agreement entered into between the landlord and SSE. However, he thought that would not be the case. Equally he could not guarantee that by going down the Part 3 route that difficulty would necessarily be overcome.

The Trust was able to employ two temporary members of staff in 2004 to help prepare for a potential community buyout of the estate. One post provided administration support for day-to-day matters, such as writing minutes, organising local meetings, production and distribution of newsletters, managing a membership database, and collating a ballot roll. The other was for undertaking mapping duties with respect to the estate's common grazings and to liaise with CnES regarding digital mapping as part of preparations for a Part 3 buyout. Funding for the posts was provided by the Scottish Land Fund (SLF) and HIE.

PREPARING FOR A PART 3 APPLICATION

The mapping requirements for Part 3 applications were particularly onerous in the author's opinion. These were outlined partly in the Act itself, partly in secondary legislation, and partly in accompanying advice from the Scottish Executive. Three maps were required:

(a) A map defining the extent and location of croft land and any other eligible land sought in the buyout. The scale of the map needed to be 1:10,000 or larger, showing boundaries in correct detail and giving the size of the area concerned 'as determined by an experienced surveyor'. The area of any significant bodies of water had to be indicated and their extent noted separately. Eligible croft land and any eligible additional land had to be separately highlighted and their specific extents noted. Any areas excluded from the land sought for purchase also had to be marked.

(b) A map indicating certain features, fixtures and improvements. The legislation specified that these should include: sewers, pipes, lines, water courses or other conduits; and fences, dykes, ditches or other boundaries in or on the land. Accompanying advice from the Scottish Executive suggested that woodland, roads, tracks, servitudes, wayleaves, rights of way and the extent of any collective rights such as peat cutting rights should also be identified on this map. Applicants were recommended to obtain the advice of a professionally qualified land agent with experience in preparing sale particulars for substantial rural properties. This map also needed to be 1:10,000 or larger scale.

(c) A map to highlight within the boundary of the land sought for purchase, any areas of land which were to be excluded from the application and the extent of all rights and interests in the land to be purchased. This map also needed to be 1:10,000 or larger scale.

The maps needed to be accompanied by an explanation of their contents, measurements of distance and a note of where these appear as part of the written content of the application.

In ensuring that the land included in the application was eligible croft land or eligible additional land, the Scottish Executive Part 3 advice stated that owner occupied crofts, crofts and croft house sites which had been decrofted, and areas of land that had been resumed from crofting tenure were not eligible croft land. The advice acknowledged that it was not always a simple matter to determine whether land is eligible croft land. However, despite this, it seemed to the Trust that the consequences of making a mistake on a matter of detail could lead to an application being rejected.

The Scottish Executive advice also recommended that a Part 3 application should include a 'comprehensive land, resources management and development plan covering the process of acquisition and, at least, the first three years following purchase'. The advice included that budgets should be developed for the period of the plan, with sources of funding identified and spend allocated between activities. Furthermore, capital costs and funding should be distinguished from annual costs and revenues; and depreciation of assets and allocations for replacements should also be shown. And, if the Trust's proposals for the use and development of land (or water) had any effect on other land beyond the boundaries of that sought to be purchased, then proposed solutions should be fully set out in the plan.

The application also had to demonstrate the extent to which the proposals in the Trust's plan would consist of or support the sustainable use or sustainable development of the land. The advice stated that 'as one of the policy aims of Part 3 of the Act is to permit crofting communities greater opportunities to achieve sustainable development, the application should show how this would be an outcome of the proposed purchase'. Furthermore, the Trust should obtain 'advice and expertise to identify the environmental assets and heritage features of the land and clearly indicate how these are to be employed, maintained or enhanced for the benefit of the community'.

THE FIRST BALLOT

Part 3 of the Act also required a ballot of all eligible members of a crofting community to be undertaken within a six-month period immediately preceding the date of a crofting community right to buy application. The crofting community had to be defined and its membership established before either a ballot was held or a subsequent application submitted. Failure to define the crofting community could result in an application failing because the ballot was found to be invalid.

Detailed advice was provided by the Scottish Executive on how to define the crofting community and identify crofting community members, and how to give notice of who may vote in a ballot. It stressed the importance of getting the definition of community membership correct given the scope for someone to attempt to thwart a right to buy application by seeking to have a ballot result declared invalid. To minimise the risk of challenge or rejection of a ballot result, the advice suggested that it might make sense to employ an independent professional to establish the membership of a local community for the purposes of the Act. The advice also recommended showing the outcome of consideration of the extent of membership of a crofting community to the Scottish Executive Environment and Rural Affairs Department (SEERAD) before a ballot was conducted.

The Act provided that a majority of the members of the community who voted in the ballot and a majority of the croft tenant members of the community who voted had to support an application for a crofting community right to buy. A ballot had to be conducted as prescribed in the Crofting Community Right to Buy (Ballot) (Scotland) Regulations 2004.

It is clear from all of the above advice that the processes leading up to a ballot were both complex and extremely time consuming. Moreover, the legislation allowed only a maximum of six months between a ballot and submission of a Part 3 application. Given this, and the various complexities involved in putting together a valid and robust application (in particular those associated with the mapping requirements), the Trust decided to confine its Part 3 application to the estate's common grazings.

This was simply a pragmatic decision, based largely on the perceived impracticality of accurately mapping all of the numerous exclusions within the in bye land within the time available. Many years later, when the Trust had to map the in bye land as part of its voluntary purchase of the whole of the estate before the land could be registered in the Trust's name, the exercise took some six months and cost several thousand pounds, even with the co-operation of the landlord and considerable assistance from Registers of Scotland. This is discussed in more detail in later chapters.

The local authority, Comhairle nan Eilean Siar (CnES) agreed to run the ballot on behalf of the community. The ballot was fixed for Monday 29 November 2004 and postal votes had to be received by CnES by 4.00pm on that day. For votes in person ballot boxes were located at Gravir Primary School in the evening between 7.00pm and 9.00pm.

The ballot question read:

Are you in favour of The Pairc Trust (company number 261145) applying to Scottish Ministers for consent to buy the common grazings and associated assets including sporting and mineral rights of Pairc Estate in Lewis using the provisions of the Land Reform (Scotland) Act 2003: Part 3, Crofting Community Right to Buy?

The official results as announced by the Deputy Returning Officer of CnES, Derek MacKay, on the evening of 29 November 2004 were:
- The number of persons eligible to vote in the ballot 379
- The number of eligible persons who did vote 256
- The number of valid votes cast 254
- The number of valid votes cast in favour 222
- The number of valid votes cast against 32

The breakdown of valid votes cast was:

TOWNSHIP VOTE (residents and crofters counted together)
- Number of persons eligible to vote 379
- Turnout 67.5%
- Yes 222 (87.4%)
- No 32 (12.6%)
- Spoilt votes 2

CROFTER VOTE (crofters only)
- Number of persons eligible to vote 149
- Turnout 77.9%
- Yes 99 (85.3%)
- No 17 (14.7%)

It is worth noting that in the information provided by the Trust to voters it was made clear that the vote was for a community buyout of the estate, not a vote for or against a wind farm. The ballot demonstrated overwhelming support for a Part 3 community buyout of the estate's common grazings (and associated assets). As required by the legislation, the approval of both the overall crofting community, and of the croft tenants, had been obtained. Over 87 per cent of those who voted (on a 67.5 per cent turnout) supported a buyout. In other words, out of every 100 people who voted, 87 supported a buyout and only 13 did not.

The Trust then proceeded to finalise a Crofting Community Right to Buy Application to the Scottish Executive, which was submitted on 27 May 2005, just within the deadline of six months. This was a ground breaking application, the very first under Part 3 of the Act and indeed the only such application made at the time of writing other than the two further applications submitted by the Trust in 2010.

CHAPTER THREE: SUMMARY AND REFLECTIONS

The decisions taken by the Trust in the summer of 2004 to proceed towards a Part 3 application for consent to purchase the estate, and to limit this application for pragmatic reasons to the common grazings, were crucial to the future history of the buyout. While discussions were still proceeding with Barry Lomas in early 2004 about a possible voluntary ('amicable') transfer of the estate, the Trust came to the view that these were leading nowhere and that the Part 3 approach was preferable. It also decided that making a Part 3 application for consent to purchase the in bye land as well as the common grazings was impractical in the immediate future, primarily because of the onerous mapping requirements which would lead to a significant delay in submitting the application.

In the author's opinion, it is entirely understandable why the Trust made these important judgements, both of which were subsequently endorsed by the community by a large majority in the ballot of November 2004. Was there any realistic prospect of the landlord agreeing to a voluntary transfer in 2004 on terms that might have been acceptable to the Pairc community? We can never know the answer to this question, but given the priority which Barry Lomas seemed to be giving during 2004 to setting up a subsidiary company (PRL) and a sub-lease between PRL and SSE to advance his plans for a commercial wind farm (the full details of which were not made available to the Trust until later), it appears unlikely that he would have settled for a purchase price which did not reflect a substantial financial return from the wind farm. It seems also likely that the Pairc Trust would have found such a price unacceptably high. There can also be no doubt that, had the Trust decided to include the in bye land in its Part 3 application, the practical difficulties of mapping this land in the detail required by the legislation and without the co-operation of the landlord would have delayed the application by many months.

While therefore these decisions by the Pairc Trust seem to be reasonable and justified, the consequences for the future were significant. Barry Lomas may have viewed the Part 3 application as being unjustified, unnecessary and even, perhaps, provocative. Any reasonable chance of a genuinely amicable agreement may have been destroyed from that point onwards forever. The relationship between the landlord and the Trust (and particularly certain directors) became openly confrontational and probably could never have been repaired – whatever the gloss put on the eventual 'voluntary transfer' agreement. From this time on, in the author's view, Barry Lomas seemed to take a number of steps to oppose what he may have seen as an unwarranted and unnecessary compulsory purchase of the estate under Part 3 of the Act. As subsequent chapters describe, he appears only to have re-entered serious discussions with the Trust about a voluntary transfer when it became clear to him that his legal attempts to challenge a Part 3 purchase were unlikely to be successful.

Confining the Part 3 application to the common grazings also had important consequences. Although the ballot result of November 2004 was overwhelmingly in favour of the Trust's proposal, a potential complexity or difficulty lay ahead for some crofters in that if a Part 3 application was successful, crofters would have two landlords for an unknown period of time – the existing landlord for the in bye land and the Pairc Trust for the common grazings. The author is aware that for a number of crofters this would have been perceived as a negative factor even though in practical terms it is unlikely (in the author's opinion) to have made much of a difference to most of them on a day to day basis. It was probably seen by some as a necessary but unwelcome consequence of going down the Part 3 route. But for some crofters, probably a small minority, it may have been an important factor in their not supporting a Part 3 application. For some in the community, the author has been told it was simply the existing landlord's continuing presence that was the problem and that is why they supported a Part 3 buyout. There was always of course the possibility that the Trust could have acquired the in bye land (and Steimreway) at a later date, either through another Part 3 application or through voluntary negotiation. No doubt this was firmly in the back of the Trust's mind though there was no guarantee that either course would happen speedily.

The Interposed Lease

NEW LEASE ARRANGEMENTS AND THEIR IMPLICATIONS

Although the details were not made known to the Pairc Trust at the time, it later became clear that the landlord and his advisers had been working during 2004 on a radically new structure of governance for the Pairc Estate. First they decided to establish a new company, Pairc Renewables Limited (PRL), which was formally incorporated on 6 August 2004. PRL was in effect a subsidiary company of Pairc Crofters Limited (PCL) and was essentially controlled (so far as the author is aware) by the same people who controlled PCL. Later the same month PCL granted a lease to PRL over the whole of the Pairc Estate, delegating to PRL all the rights which PCL had previously exercised over the estate apart from sporting rights (which PCL retained). The lease was for seventy-five years, from 6 August 2004 to 5 August 2079 (and thereafter from year to year until terminated by either party, giving not less than twelve months written notice). An annual rent of £1,000 was payable by PRL to PCL.

In November 2004, PRL granted a sub lease over the estate to Scottish and Southern Electricity Generation Ltd (SSE) to allow it (subject to the necessary consents) to develop a wind farm. The lease between PCL and PRL specifically provided for a sub lease of the whole or part of the Pairc Estate to SSE. The sub lease between PRL and SSE was for a period of twenty-five years, expiring on 28 February 2029. An initial rent of £1,000 per annum was to be payable by SSE during the early years of the sub lease, while planning permission was being obtained. That initial rent was to increase to £2,000 per annum if planning permission had not been obtained within five years and SSE wanted the sub-lease to continue. Once the necessary permissions were in place a rent based on the installed generating capacity of the potential wind farm was to be payable by SSE to PRL. This would have been a potentially significantly much larger sum than the nominal fixed figure of £1,000 per annum which was to be payable by PRL to PCL for the seventy-five years' duration of the interposed lease.

The lease between PCL and PRL and the sub lease between PRL and SSE made the previous arrangements under the Option Agreement between PCL and SSE redundant. Although proceeding by way of an Option Agreement would have been the norm, the position for both PCL and SSE was complicated by the fact that the landowner, PCL, could have had the land which was the subject of the negotiations with SSE, taken away from it compulsorily by virtue of Part 3 of the Land Reform (Scotland) Act 2003. If that were to happen, PCL might no longer have been in a position to implement its contractual obligations to SSE under the Option Agreement. That being the case, SSE may have concluded that it should seek some other means of safeguarding its position. It could, therefore, have been in the interest of both PCL and SSE to put a formal lease in place at an earlier stage than normal. That would, arguably, have helped PCL by increasing the value of the estate if it were to be bought by the community, and would also give SSE greater security as tenant under an actual lease, rather than holding a contractual right to take a lease from a landowner who, when the time came, might not have been in a position to grant it.

The lease arrangement between PCL and PRL was what is known as an interposed lease. This was a relatively new form of lease in Scotland, having been permitted by Section 17 of the Land Tenure (Scotland) Act 1974. An interposed lease allowed a landlord to grant a lease of land already leased, for a longer or shorter period than an existing lease (or for the same duration) but subject to the existing lease. The new interest is referred to as an interposed lease.

It was because of the longstanding, pre-existing let of the croft land to crofters on the Pairc Estate that the lease to PRL was said to be 'interposed'. It was put in place between PCL and the crofters' existing rights to occupy the land derived through various Crofting

Acts. By creating the interposed lease, PCL could not diminish the existing rights of the crofters, but it transferred its own rights to act as the crofters' landlord to PRL. Whilst the lease gave PRL no greater rights than PCL had held in relation to the crofters on the estate, PCL lost its rights in relation to them in exchange for the right to receive a rent from PRL. However, the crofters' pre-existing and exclusive rights to occupy the land had to be respected by PRL.

PCL leased the whole of the Pairc Estate to PRL with only one exception – that of the sporting rights – which it retained. Due to the terms in the interposed lease, the rights which PCL could exercise as the owner of the land were hugely diluted and virtually extinguished. Although PCL remained the owner of the land, the terms of the lease meant that, effectively, PRL assumed full control of the estate. In return for this privilege PRL had to pay PCL only a nominal annual rent. The interposed lease did not provide for the retention by PCL of any rights which would have allowed it to carry out any developments on the let land at any time in the future, during the lifetime of the interposed lease, without the consent of PRL.

The view of the Trust was that the underlying purpose of PCL in putting the interposed lease in place, was to try to ensure that, even if the Pairc Trust was to purchase PCL's interests as owner of the Pairc Estate, the income generated from the estate, and in particular the potentially significant income which would be generated by the development of a wind farm of the magnitude which SSE was understood to have in mind, would remain in the hands of the Lomas family through its control of PRL.

The implications of the interposed lease and sub lease did not become clear to the Trust until well after the November 2004 ballot and its Part 3 application submission in May 2005. The sub lease was not signed until 26 November 2004, a mere three days before the public ballot, and the Trust was not formally notified of the creation of the interposed lease (but with no mention of the sub lease) until February 2005.

A crucial consequence of the interposed lease (assuming it was legally valid – a question which was only finally determined by the Land Court in 2007) was that if the Pairc Trust had bought the common grazings without purchasing the interests of PRL as tenant under that lease, then it would have found itself in the same position as PCL – that is, owner of the land but without any control over it. In essence, without the lease, the Trust would have needed PRL's agreement to almost every proposed development it wished to pursue. It would also have restricted the right of the Trust to that of receiving the nominal annual rent that had been payable by PRL to PCL – allowing no other significant income streams without PRL's agreement.

Control and management of the estate (which is what the Trust was seeking to achieve through the buyout), therefore, would have remained in the hands of PRL – making a buyout of only PCL's interest an almost completely pointless exercise from the Trust's point of view as well as being a waste of public money. There could be no guarantee that PRL's agreement would have been forthcoming to any of the Trust's proposals – or, if so, on what terms. It eventually became clear, therefore, that it was essential that the Trust should be able (and needed) to acquire the interposed lease, along with the land, if it wanted to promote any sort of meaningful economic and social development on the estate.

All of the time the sub-lease between PRL and SSE was in place, the Trust would have had to live with this inherited obligation even if it purchased the rights of PRL in the interposed lease. Only if SSE had been prepared to renegotiate the sub lease, or if it was voluntarily terminated by the two parties, would the Trust not have been subject to its terms (that is the rights which PRL had sub let to SSE). These terms related only to wind farm developments.

The right of PRL to receive other income from the estate extended beyond that which could be derived from a wind farm. However, these other income streams at the time the lease was established (for example, croft rents) were relatively small. Without doubt, it was the prospect of a large, commercial wind farm which potentially transformed the value of the interposed lease to a completely higher order of magnitude.

The mere creation of the interposed lease did not add any value to the interest which PCL had held before the granting of the lease. What it did, was to transfer most of the value, including hope value, of what PCL had held to PRL. If there had been no interposed lease the value of the estate in the hands of PCL would have been the same, with the hope value fluctuating according to the prospects of the wind farm being consented and becoming operational.

The Pairc Estate was not the only case at the time where the owner of croft land had formed a new company to which the estate then leased the land asset through an interposed lease – and, in turn, with that new company then granting a sub-lease to a wind farm developer. A similar situation had arisen at Galson in the north-west of Lewis where the local community was pursuing a buyout. There, Galson Estate Ltd was negotiating a 109-year lease to a new company controlled by it – Galson Energy Ltd.

These developments were causing considerable concern in several quarters – including Highlands and Islands Enterprise (HIE) and the Scottish Government (prior to 2007 known as the Scottish Executive) – especially as there were some doubts being expressed (not least by the Pairc Trust and its legal advisers) regarding the legal validity of interposed leases over croft land and also the effect they would have on any proposed purchases by crofting communities under Part 3 of the Land Reform (Scotland) Act 2003. It was widely suspected that the purpose of the creation of interposed leases by private landowners was, in the main, to try to prevent the financial benefit derived from wind farm developments passing to crofting communities on their becoming landowners on completion of a land buyout.

If interposed leases were valid over croft land, then, arguably, there was very little public benefit to be had in community ownership of land that had been leased to a third party. It would also be difficult for HIE and the Scottish Land Fund (SLF) to financially support community buyouts in such circumstances. And it would be onerous for crofting community bodies to satisfy the requirements of Part 3 of the Act that applications should be compatible with furthering the achievement of sustainable development and that the land purchase was in the public interest.

In order to help clarify matters, HIE sought legal opinion on the matter. It commissioned advice from Roderick Paisley, Professor of Commercial Property Law at the University of Aberdeen. His report was received towards the end of September 2005 and made publicly available the following month (before Scottish Ministers took the case to the Land Court). Professor Paisley's view was that interposed leases were void without the consent of the Crofters Commission under the Crofters (Scotland) Act 1993, section 23 (3). This proved to be wrong. However, the matter was only finally resolved by a legal decision which did not support Professor Paisley's view, after Scottish Ministers referred the validity of such leases to the Land Court for a determination.

REFERRAL TO THE SCOTTISH LAND COURT

Later in 2005, using the Pairc Estate as a test case, Scottish Ministers decided it was essential to obtain a ruling from the Scottish Land Court (SLC) – which has the jurisdiction in terms of the 2003 Act – as to the validity of the interposed lease; and also on the question of what exactly a Crofting Community Body (CCB) could buy in terms of Part 3 of the 2003 Act. This move was very much supported by the Pairc Trust, believing the interposed lease to be invalid and that it had been constructed to circumvent the right of the community to take effective control and management of the estate.

However, before that, in June 2005, the Scottish Executive Environment and Rural Affairs Department (SEERAD) wrote to all interested parties inviting them to submit their views on the Trust's Part 3 application within sixty days. PCL objected to the application on several grounds, claiming that:

- It was 'incompetent' in a number of ways, stating, for example, that it was full of inaccuracies and that several voters ought to have been excluded from the ballot;
- It included lochs and water courses but that these did not fall within the definition of 'eligible croft land' in section 68 or 'additional land' in section 70 of the 2003 Act;
- It was not compatible with furthering the achievement of sustainable development as required by section 74 of the 2003 Act, particularly because the lease set up by PCL and sub-lease by PRL precluded the Trust from any effective management of the land beyond receiving the low rents from the estate's crofters. Furthermore, PCL claimed that the Trust's business plan did not support sustainable development, even if the Trust had full management of the land;
- It was not in the public interest because the exclusion of the Trust from any effective management of the land meant that there was no public interest in the acquisition. Furthermore, even if the Trust had full management of the land, its business plan would not be able to support sustainable development and therefore the application was not in the public interest.

In addition, PCL reserved the right to challenge the competence of Part 3 of the 2003 Act on the grounds that it was not compatible with the European Convention on Human Rights as required by section 29 of the Scotland Act 1998.

SEERAD sent copies of PCL's views to the Pairc Trust, inviting it to submit its counter response. This it duly did, with input from Roy Shearer.

Once Scottish Ministers had referred matters to the SLC, effectively the Trust's Part 3 application was put on hold pending the court's decision. This caused a considerable delay as that decision was not forthcoming until August 2007. The SLC considered two questions posed by Scottish Ministers:

(a) Whether, in the absence of the consent of the Crofters Commission in terms of section 23 (3) of the Crofters (Scotland) Act 1993, interposed leases were valid or not; and

(b) If they were valid, what were the nature and extent of the interests which could be acquired by the Pairc Trust under section 73 of the 2003 Act.

It considered one further question put to it by PCL and PRL:

(c) Whether the lochs and water courses lying within the general geographical area of the common grazings sought to be acquired by the Pairc Trust were 'eligible croft land' in terms of section 68 of the 2003 Act.

The questions were eventually debated in the Land Court in a hearing lasting two days on 12 and 13 June 2007. Scottish Ministers, PCL (and therefore PRL) and the Pairc Trust were all represented. SSE submitted a letter indicating its support for the validity of the leases but took no further part in procedures – their interests essentially subsumed within those of PCL and PRL.

The SLC issued its decision on 15 August 2007. It decided:

• Absence of consent by the Crofters Commission did not invalidate interposed leases and, therefore, they were valid in a crofting context. This meant that a landlord could create an interposed lease, standing between itself and its crofting tenants; and

• In terms of section 73 of the 2003 Act, the Pairc Trust could acquire an owner's eligible land subject to the rights of third parties such as crofters, interposed leases and other lessees. This meant that the effect of the 2003 Act was simply to put a Crofting Community Body (CCB), such as the Pairc Trust, in place of a landlord, and that a CCB would therefore acquire the land not only with all of the rights, but also subject to all of the obligations attached to it; and

- Subject to any relevant history as to the status of any particular stretch of water, loch or water courses lying within a common grazing, they will fall to be treated as eligible croft land within the meaning of section 73 of the 2003 Act. The SLC, therefore, rejected PCL's argument that stretches of water, lochs or water courses on a common grazing were not 'eligible land'. Whilst in some cases whether or not a particular body of water was part of a common grazing would be a question of fact, subject to such exceptions, as a matter of law 'eligible croft land' included them and they would pass to a CCB (in this case the Pairc Trust) on completion of a buyout.

In fact, the problems created by the interposed lease for land reform policy were resolved prior to the Land Court's decision. This was done by an amendment to the 2003 Act, introduced as part of the Crofting Reform etc (Scotland) Act 2007. This allowed a CCB to buy out any such lease granted by a landlord. The matter was clearly regarded by Scottish Ministers as sufficiently serious to promote the amending legislation in order to close the potential loophole in the 2003 Act, without waiting for the Land Court's decision on the Pairc Estate test case. Nevertheless, the Land Court's ruling was important in clarifying, beyond any doubt, the situation regarding the legality specifically of interposed leases in a crofting situation.

Some sections of the media took the view that the Trust had lost its case and that the Land Court's decision was a major setback. This opinion was not shared by the Trust. It viewed, instead, the Land Court's decision as bringing to an end arguments as to what could or could not be included in a buyout; and to allow the Trust to proceed with its Part 3 application, including the interposed lease between PCL and PRL – and to continue with its acquisition of lochs and watercourses on the estate's common grazings.

CHAPTER FOUR: SUMMARY AND REFLECTIONS

The landlord's establishment of an interposed lease between PCL and PRL, together with the sub lease between PRL and SSE, introduced major complications for the Pairc Trust's attempt to buy the estate on behalf of the community. It was perhaps the single most important factor contributing to the long delay in the Trust being able to acquire the estate. While it can be argued that a formal lease between the owner of the Pairc Estate and SSE (rather than an Option Agreement) was necessary to give SSE the security it needed to proceed with the proposed wind farm development, the effect of the interposed lease between PCL and PRL was to place an obstacle in the way of meeting the intentions of Part 3 of the Land Reform (Scotland) Act 2003; and in particular the Pairc Trust's right to purchase and exercise effective control and management over the estate on behalf of the local community. The fact that the Government decided to refer the matter to the Scottish Land Court for a judgement on the legality of interposed leases, using the Pairc example as a test case, is evidence of the importance that the Scottish Government attached to the issue.

The decision of the Scottish Land Court, while confirming the legality of interposed leases, was helpful in clarifying the position, and in demonstrating that the Pairc Trust would need to purchase the interests of PRL in the interposed lease and as a consequence take over PRL's rights under the sub lease with SSE, as well as those of PCL as the landowner, if it was to exercise the normal powers of a landlord over the estate. This conclusion had already been anticipated by the decision of the Scottish Parliament earlier in 2007 to amend Part 3 of the Act to make it explicit that Crofting Community Bodies such as the Pairc Trust could acquire the rights of a tenant in an interposed lease.

The interposed lease delayed the community buyout in two important respects. First, the referral of the matter to the Scottish Land Court took almost two years to resolve. Secondly, the need for the Pairc Trust to apply to purchase the interposed lease, as well as the land, made the process of applying under Part 3 of the Act even more complicated than before – and eventually led to the Trust submitting in 2010 two new Part 3 applications (effectively overtaking the original Part 3 application of 2005). In spite of

having to start the Part 3 process all over again, the fact that the
2003 Act had been amended meant that the possibility of the
community being able to gain meaningful management control
of the estate by the Part 3 route had actually been strengthened.
In the short run, this encouraged the Trust to devote more effort
to persuading the landlord to agree to a voluntary transfer of the
whole of Pairc. It appeared to the Trust that the prospect of Barry
Lomas being able to retain any meaningful control of the estate had
been so diminished that it was hoped he might be more amenable to
a voluntary transfer.

CHAPTER FIVE

Exploring the Scope for a Voluntary Transfer

RECONSIDERING THE OPTIONS

Following the Scottish Land Court's decision in August 2007 on the interposed lease and associated issues, there was a prolonged period marked by a number of unsuccessful attempts by the Pairc Trust to negotiate with Barry Lomas a mutually acceptable voluntary transfer of the Pairc Estate and the lease between PCL and PRL. At a public meeting at Pairc School on 14 September 2007, the Trust outlined three possible options:

> (1) Continuing with a Part 3 land buyout without purchasing the interposed lease;
>
> (2) Purchasing the interposed lease through an amended Part 3 application;
>
> (3) Purchasing the land and the interposed lease through a negotiated voluntary settlement with PCL.

Its preferred option, stated at the public meeting, was the purchase of the interposed lease through either option (2) or (3). The Trust explained that, at a meeting with Barry Lomas on 1 September 2007 he had indicated a willingness to enter into a negotiated settlement – followed up by a written statement to that effect received from him on the day of the public meeting.

Because there were no precedents in relation to Part 3 applications, there were procedural uncertainties as to whether or not the

Trust could amend its May 2005 Part 3 application to include the interposed lease; or if the 2003 Act required submission of new Part 3 applications covering both the land and the interposed lease.

The Trust asked those present at the meeting to support its recommendation to attempt to purchase the interposed lease through either option (2) or (3). This was agreed 'with applause' – though no vote was taken. In practice, options (2) and (3) – a compulsory purchase of both the land and lease using Part 3 of the 2003 Act or a negotiated voluntary transfer of both the land and lease – were not mutually exclusive. Both were capable of being pursued simultaneously in a twin track approach by the Trust if it wished to do so. It is important to note, however, that option (3) could have covered, in principle, purchase of the whole estate (including the in bye land), whereas option (2), through an amended Part 3 application, would have been confined to the common grazings as in the original 2005 application.

DEVELOPMENTS WITH THE COMMERCIAL WIND FARM PROPOSAL

A crucial backdrop to the Trust's consideration of the options was the changing nature of the commercial wind farm proposal on the Pairc Estate drawn up by SSE under its lease with PRL. Although the proposal had been under informal discussion and development by SSE for a long time, the first formal application was lodged by SSE with the Scottish Government, under Section 36 of the Electricity Act 1989, in July 2007. This was for a wind farm of fifty-seven turbines with a total generating capacity of 205 MW annually over twenty-five years. CnES was the principal consultee and it, in turn, gathered comments from numerous other organisations on the island (including community councils) before submitting its views to Scottish Government in December 2007. It recommended that Scottish Ministers approve a much reduced scheme for twenty-six turbines (subject to numerous terms and conditions).

As a result of these consultations, and in line with CnES recommendations, thirty-one of the fifty-seven turbines were excluded by SSE from the scheme. SSE submitted a revised application to Scottish Government (technically an addendum to the original application) over a year later, in early February 2009 for a wind farm of twenty-six turbines with a total generating capacity of 94 MW annually over twenty-five years.

This proposal, if approved by the Scottish Government, still promised to provide a very substantial income stream to the Estate (through PRL) over the lifetime of the wind farm. The hope value of the interposed lease – at least in the view of the landlord – was increased very significantly once an application had been submitted to the Scottish Government at the end of 2007; and again when a revised smaller scheme was lodged in early 2009 with the support of the local authority.

Indeed, discussions between the Trust and Barry Lomas suggested that he was thinking in terms of a value for the Estate well in excess of what an independent valuation would have probably produced – even though related decisions such as construction of a new inter-connector cable to take the island's electricity to the mainland grid had yet to be taken. As it transpired (see later chapters), the SSE application was not approved by Scottish Ministers, but during 2009 the prospect of such a major development – albeit reduced in scale from the original application – appeared very real.

FAILURE OF DISCUSSIONS ON A VOLUNTARY TRANSFER

Taking account of this changing background, the Trust chose initially to explore the possibility of a voluntary transfer of the whole estate. A key meeting was held in March 2009 with Barry Lomas, representatives of Scottish Government and HIE. While the meeting appeared to be positive and resulted in a new timetable working towards a voluntary transfer of the estate, the first agreed milestone along that route – provision of information to the company (Bidwells) commissioned (in December 2008) by HIE to provide a valuation of the estate – was not met by PCL. That independent valuation still went ahead despite the landowner's lack of co-operation. It is worth noting that the valuation (although a confidential document) indicated a valuation for the land and interposed lease which was considerably lower than what the landlord was seeking.

The Trust made a further (unsuccessful) attempt to negotiate a voluntary transfer with Barry Lomas in the summer of 2009. A meeting was held with him in June in Edinburgh at Scottish Government offices. The Trust was represented by its then chairman Donald Murdo Maclennan (a crofter and fish farm manager from the crofting township of Marvig who had succeeded Donald John

Macdonald as chairman in early 2009) and vice chairman Angus McDowall. Heather Holmes, a civil servant from the Scottish Government (renamed from the former Scottish Executive in 2007), also attended the meeting. The Trust had provided Barry Lomas with written details of its Board's proposals prior to the day of the meeting.

However, during discussions, Barry Lomas rejected the proposals at the morning's meeting. In an attempt to keep the dialogue going in relation to a possible voluntary agreement, Donald Murdo Maclennan and Angus McDowall put together amended proposals for further discussion with him in the afternoon. They were keen to keep the possibility of a voluntary transfer alive, rather than seeing the talks collapse so that a return to Part 3 would be inevitable. The amended proposals, whilst resulting in Barry Lomas agreeing to continue the discussions, were also not acceptable to him as they stood. But when Donald Murdo Maclennan and Angus McDowall reported back to the Trust's board a few days later, the amended proposals did not receive its unanimous support. According to the Trust, Barry Lomas then accused it of back tracking on its position, having wrongly assumed (according to the Trust) that the amended proposals had received the backing of the full board over the lunchtime period before the meeting resumed in the afternoon in Edinburgh. So, discussions about a voluntary transfer came to an end for the time being amidst some acrimony, with Barry Lomas, according to the Trust, accusing it of having reneged on its proposals. Donald Murdo Maclennan stood down from the Trust at the September 2009 annual general meeting for personal reasons, having completed his three-year term as a director.

RETURNING TO PART 3

By July 2009, therefore, the Trust felt that it had no option but to reactivate its application under Part 3 of the Land Reform Act to acquire both the estate and the interposed lease. It reached a decision, in its view, that Barry Lomas was not really interested in a voluntary transfer (of the land and interposed lease) at a price and on terms that were acceptable to the Trust (and therefore, by implication, to the local community). The judgement was made by the Pairc Trust that he was simply, in its words, 'stringing us along', waiting for the commercial wind farm application to be approved so that the price of the estate would increase significantly. Barry

Lomas had also been insistent that, as part of any voluntary transfer deal, the Trust should formally withdraw its 2005 Part 3 application. This was a step which would have opened the way for him to make a compensation claim against the Trust under the terms of the 2003 Act, and which the Trust was unwilling to take. The Trust therefore decided to pursue a Part 3 application whilst at the same time leaving the door open for further negotiations towards a voluntary transfer. Indeed, the Part 3 route was seen, by the Trust, as the only meaningful lever available to it to bring about an acceptable deal (to it and the local community) through a voluntary transfer.

There was prolonged debate within the Trust about whether its existing Part 3 application could and should be amended; or if new applications – which would, inter alia, include the interposed lease – were required. Advice from Scottish Government officials was that new applications should be submitted and another ballot held. This was for three main reasons:

(a) It was approaching five years since the first ballot had been held and therefore that meant community support for a buyout should be retested;

(b) Importantly, the 2005 ballot had made no explicit reference to the interposed lease; and

(c) The 2005 application was, in the view of government officials, deficient – not least because without acquiring the interposed lease the sustainable development test (required by the 2003 Act) would not be met.

The lack of reference by the Trust to the interposed lease in the 2005 ballot was quite understandable – and in reality unavoidable – given the timing of both. Furthermore, the legality and full implications of the interposed lease were not clear until after amendments were made to the Land Reform (Scotland) Act 2003 and following the Scottish Land Court's judgement in 2007. Both made it clear that from that point onwards a landlord's interests in such leases could be purchased by crofting community bodies.

If the Trust had ignored the advice given by government officials it is likely that it would have opened itself to legal challenge by the landlord, particularly on the absence of a reference to the interposed lease in the 2004 ballot and in the Trust's 2005 Part 3 application. At the same time, the financial climate which the Trust found itself in after 2007 became progressively more and more difficult. In particular this was due to the abolition of a dedicated Scottish Land Fund for land purchases; and also the need for the Trust to compete against other projects for diminishing resources from the Big Lottery Fund on criteria which did not give priority to land purchases.

In line with advice from Scottish Government officials, therefore, the Trust decided to hold a further ballot of the community with a view to submitting two new Part 3 applications – one for consent to purchase the common grazings, and the other for consent to purchase the interposed lease (formally to purchase the rights of the tenant, PRL, in the interposed lease).

It should be noted that the increasing likelihood at the time of a commercial wind farm on the Pairc Estate also caused the Trust to devote substantial time and effort during this period to another main task, namely maximising the community benefit that could arise from it. In conjunction with other local organisations such as Kinloch Community Council (from parts of which area the wind farm would be visible) and the Western Isles Development Trust (which had close links with CnES and sought to spread the benefits from wind farms to all parts of the Western Isles), the Trust sought to persuade SSE that it should amend its standard criteria for community benefit in order to increase the benefits for communities in Lewis because of the area's special needs. However, this was resisted by SSE. The Trust believed that SSE generally showed less sensitivity to local concerns than other wind farm development companies active in the Outer Hebrides. The author has been told that, unlike some other developers, SSE did not have an office or official located in Lewis to act as a contact point for the local communities, and that it demonstrated less flexibility than other wind farm companies in its approach to the calculation of community benefit, keeping to a standard model which made little allowance for differences in the Outer Hebrides. The Trust also engaged in considerable (ultimately unproductive) discussion about how any community benefit from the Pairc wind farm should be shared out between the Pairc Trust (for Pairc), Kinloch Community Council (for Kinloch), and the Western Isles Development Trust (for the Western Isles as a whole).

Before the December 2009 ballot the Trust made one final (but unsuccessful) attempt to reach a voluntary transfer agreement with Barry Lomas. The new chairman Angus McDowall and vice chairman John Randall met Barry Lomas in Birmingham on 26 November 2009 to discuss a new proposal which had been agreed by the Trust's board. The board's feeling was that, even at this eleventh hour, it was worth seeing if Barry Lomas was open to voluntary transfer terms which might be acceptable to the Pairc community – and that with a Part 3 ballot imminent the timing gave the Trust maximum leverage to secure a negotiated voluntary settlement.

The underlying principle behind this new proposal was to use income which the Trust would have received from the SSE wind farm (assuming this went ahead and the Trust became the landlord and head tenant of the interposed lease) to purchase the estate. However, the discussions were unsuccessful and so the community ballot went ahead in the hope that its outcome would approve the submission by the Trust of two new Part 3 applications.

CHAPTER FIVE: SUMMARY AND REFLECTIONS

The period 2007 – 2009 was important in at least three respects:

First, the advantages and disadvantages of a voluntary transfer or a Part 3 approach really began to crystallise in the minds of Pairc Trust board members. Each board member probably had his or her own thoughts on the best strategy to achieve ownership of the estate. Resolving the way ahead was a gradual iterative process, no doubt varying for each director. It was also probably during this period that the seeds were sown of a future difference of view of approach within the board, in particular between one director and the rest. The 'twin track' approach was publicly enunciated for the first time during this period and became an explicit part of the Trust's future public narrative.

Second, the Trust established a much better relationship with Scottish Government and HIE officials. Rather than seeing them as an obstacle or part of the problem, most (but not all) board members began to have more confidence that the government would support the Trust if it heeded the advice being given by government officials and if the Trust presented a convincing case for a Part 3 community buyout in accordance with the legislation. Equally, government officials probably came to recognise and welcome what they saw as a more responsible and professional attitude on behalf of the Trust.

Third, the Trust embarked on a conscious effort to get wider public opinion on its side through a series of news releases which provided a more consistent and positive account of what it was trying to achieve. This appeared to work – as evidenced by supportive reports and editorials in newspapers and other media throughout Scotland and particularly the Highlands. It also manifested itself in the form of assistance from the emerging group which eventually formed Community Land Scotland as an umbrella body to promote community land ownership.

In the process of achieving this, the Trust probably made relations with Barry Lomas worse due to the adverse publicity he received. Also, the higher public media profile of the Trust may have intensified opposition from some parts of the local community – especially those who were anti-wind farms and also individuals who were against compulsory (as opposed to voluntary) purchase of the estate.

Amongst the substantive issues which came to the fore during this period and which were to recur in the future were:

- What to do about the large area of the Steimreway grazings which were excluded both from the 2005 Part 3 application and the subsequent 2010 applications – because the land in question was not in crofting tenure, having been let on two agricultural tenancies. The Steimreway grazings were important in several respects. First, they were the proposed location of twelve of the twenty-six planned SSE commercial wind farm turbines. Second, they also contain the ruins of the former cleared and subsequently land raided and temporarily re-occupied settlement of Steimreway. This is of great historic and iconic significance to the Pairc community today. So, for both economic and symbolic reasons, it was felt both by the Trust and many members of the local community to be highly desirable to include Steimreway in the land purchase package.

  It might in fact have proved possible for the Trust to have included Steimreway in its 2005 and 2010 Part 3 applications as 'eligible additional land' as it is contiguous to the eligible croft land and in the same ownership. However, this would have required the agreement of the landlord. This was not sought by the Trust because it thought such an agreement was unlikely to be forthcoming. In such circumstances where agreement is not possible there is provision in the Act for Ministers to refer the matter to the Land Court for resolution. It was felt by the Trust, however, that going down this route would have delayed and over complicated an already complex Part 3 application.

• Securing ownership of the Pairc foreshore was also important to the Trust and local community because of the potential future income that might be generated by the demand for piers, wayleaves, fish farms and utility lines etc. And, although the Trust had no particular projects of its own in mind at the time, there was a general feeling that the foreshore was a potentially significant economic asset which should, therefore, be in community ownership if at all possible. However, right up until close to the date of the actual purchase of the estate it was not clear who actually owned the foreshore around the Pairc Estate. Barry Lomas thought he did, but, according to the Trust, was unable to prove this. Also there seemed to be no evidence that the Crown Estate had given up any of its rights to the foreshore. Only when the Crown Estate confirmed that it had no legal interest in the Pairc foreshore in 2015 (see chapter eight) was it clear that the Pairc Trust could acquire the foreshore along with the rest of the estate.

• The other land excluded from the Part 3 application was, of course, the in bye land. This was excluded because of the difficulty of accurately and correctly mapping it. If the in bye land could be purchased too, via a voluntary transfer, this could generate income for the Trust from the de-crofting of house sites etc. It would also avoid the complication of a Part 3 application of crofters having two landlords for an unspecified even if temporary period.

A Return to Part 3

THE SECOND BALLOT

The second ballot was a postal one which closed at 6.00pm on 10 December 2009. The conduct of the ballot was contracted out by the Trust as before to the Western Isles Council (Comhairle nan Eilean Siar – CnES) in order to ensure professional and independent procedures were followed. The Trust initially approached both the Electoral Reform Society and CnES for quotations so that the ballot would be conducted independently and in line with best practice procedures. The Trust accepted the quote from CnES. The Deputy Returning Officer for CnES was Derek MacKay who once again took charge of the ballot.

Before the ballot took place the Trust held a series of public meetings in order to explain the issues. The question (the framing of which was the responsibility of the Trust) on the ballot paper was:

Are you in favour of the Pairc Trust applying to Scottish Ministers for consent to buy the common grazings of the Pairc Estate on Lewis [a map was enclosed with ballot papers], together with the mineral and sporting rights associated with this land, and the interests of Pairc Renewables Ltd through the interposed lease from Pairc Crofters Ltd in relation to this land, using the provisions of Part 3 of the Land Reform (Scotland) Act 2003?

The breakdown of the vote was:

TOWNSHIP VOTE (residents and crofters counted together)

- The number of persons eligible to vote in the ballot   376
- The number of eligible persons who did vote   282
  (75 per cent turnout)
- The number of valid votes cast   282
  (100 per cent)
- The number of valid votes cast in favour   195
  (69 per cent)
- The number of valid votes cast against   87
  (31 per cent)

CROFTER VOTE (crofters only)

- The number of persons eligible to vote in the ballot   137
- The number of eligible persons who did vote   105
  (77 per cent)
- The number of valid votes cast   105
  (100 per cent)
- The number of valid votes cast in favour   76
  (72 per cent)
- The number of valid votes cast against   29
  (28 per cent)

As in 2004, there was a substantial majority in favour of the Pairc Trust's proposal, although a comparison between the 2004 and 2009 ballot is interesting. The key points being:

- The overall turnout increased quite significantly between 2004 and 2009 – up from 67.5 per cent in 2004 to 75 per cent in 2009;
- Overall support in the community for the buyout fell markedly between 2004 and 2009 – down from 87.4 per cent in 2004 to 69 per cent in 2009;
- Crofter support for the buyout also fell markedly between 2004 and 2009, though less sharply – down from 85.3 per cent in 2004 to 72 per cent in 2009.

The increased overall turnout to 75 per cent in 2009 demonstrated a very healthy democracy at work and a significant (and increased) interest in the subject matter amongst the local community. Even though overall support for a Part 3 buyout decreased significantly, an overwhelming majority of the local community remained in favour – at 69 per cent of the total township vote and even higher at 72 per cent amongst crofters.

The reduction in support may have been due to increased opposition to a commercial wind farm; or a feeling of fatigue and frustration that the whole process of purchasing the estate was becoming too contentious, complex, and drawn out – and that possibly the Pairc Trust was responsible for some of this. Despite the obstacles in the Trust's path and the slow rate of progress towards achieving meaningful control of the estate, it is worth noting that nevertheless community support held up remarkably well over the five year period between the two ballots (November 2004 to December 2009) for acquisition via a Part 3 application.

THE TRUST'S 2010 PART 3 APPLICATIONS

The Scottish Government confirmed to the Trust in a letter dated 21 December 2009 that the ballot had been conducted in accordance with Section 75 of the Land Reform (Scotland) Act 2003 and the Crofting Community Right to Buy (Scotland) Regulations 2004. This paved the way for the Trust to then proceed to submit to Scottish Government two separate and new Part 3 applications which it did at the end of February 2010. One application was for consent to buy eligible croft land comprising most of the estate's common grazings (as with the 2005 application). The other application was for consent to buy the interest of the tenant (PRL) in tenanted land (namely PRL's rights over the same land as a result of the interposed lease). It was necessary to submit two separate (but inter linked) applications due to the legislative requirements of the 2003 Act.

It was essential to the Trust that Ministers should approve both applications. To have received approval of an application for the land alone would not have given the Trust sufficient powers to carry out its plans for sustainable development. It was also not possible under the legislation to be granted approval to purchase the interest of the tenant in the lease without also gaining consent to purchase the land.

The reason for excluding the in bye land from the application (as with the first Part 3 application of 2005) was again a pragmatic response to the onerous and time consuming mapping requirements of the legislation. The Trust still planned that in due course the community would purchase the in bye land too, either through a voluntary transfer or through a further Part 3 application.

Accompanying the two applications – and to support them – were the Trust's two Sustainable Development Statements and Business Plan. The Statement of Sustainable Development for the land application stated that, without acquiring the interest of the tenant in the associated land it would not be possible for the Trust to be able to further sustainable development given the existence of the interposed lease and the nature and characteristics of the Pairc Estate.

The Business Plan presented the Trust's proposals for sustainable development in the Pairc area and set out a strategy to support the Trust's aims of reversing population decline, creating employment, encouraging tourism and a number of other initiatives. Proposals also included a community-owned wind farm of two to four medium sized turbines. An initial feasibility study (which considered technical and financial criteria) carried out for the Trust in November 2009 by sustainable energy consultants (Sgurr Energy) concluded that such a scheme was technically and economically feasible. The research indicated that a community wind farm of this scale could achieve an annual income stream of around £1.5 million for twenty-five years on a capital investment of some £6 million. This was a quite separate proposal from the commercial wind farm proposal and would be wholly community-owned and run.

The Trust also identified good prospects for generating income on a smaller scale from three micro-hydro projects on the estate (in line with Government policy and incentives at the time) even if the community wind farm proposal did not proceed. This was based on a feasibility study funded by Community Energy Scotland in which the Trust was participating in February 2010 relating to small scale hydro electric schemes in Lewis and Harris. However, it was unable to proceed to more detailed development proposals due, according to the Trust, to the landlord refusing access to the sites in Pairc which had emerged as promising locations.

Other proposals – forming key components of the area's regeneration – in the Business Plan in the first decade of the estate being in community ownership, included:

- Ten new housing units;
- Eight jobs within the Trust itself; and
- A number of tourism initiatives to promote the area in terms of its untapped historical, natural and leisure-related

resources and opportunities. The aim was to extend the present limited infrastructure in order to deliver benefits for existing community bodies, businesses and residents. One specific project was for a camper van site, judged by the Trust (following research into facilities offered by similar initiatives elsewhere on the islands and mainland Scotland) to be economically viable.

It was not possible for the Trust to finalise the Business Plan in consultation with the community until the Scottish Government had taken decisions on its two Part 3 applications and a purchase price for the land and the lease was known. However, the Trust had consulted the community on projects, and its financial projections were based, it stated, on reliable sources, taking account of information from other community run estates in the Hebrides.

Discussions had also taken place – before submission of the Part 3 applications in 2010 – between the Trust and SSE about amending the terms of the sub lease (between PRL and SSE) should the Trust be successful in acquiring the interest of PRL. Although it had not been possible to finalise these discussions until the interest of PRL had been acquired, the Trust was confident from discussions with SSE that the company would work closely and favourably with it in this eventuality.

On submission of the two new Part 3 applications, Scottish Ministers had firstly to satisfy themselves that the Trust was properly constituted as a crofting community body and had followed the legislative procedures required to enable applications for consent to exercise the right to buy to be made. Once satisfied on these matters, the next stage in the application process was for Ministers to seek the views of interested parties on the Trust's applications. The statutory sixty day consultation period was triggered on 17 March 2010 by Ministers sending out invitations to interested parties, who had until 16 May 2010 to submit comments objecting to, or supporting, the Trust's applications. Thereafter, the Trust had the opportunity under the legislation to respond to any comments submitted.

THE LANDLORD'S PETITION FOR JUDICIAL REVIEW

However, this timetable was disrupted because of action taken by the landlord. On 30 April 2010, Barry Lomas, who was of course one of the parties invited by Ministers to comment on the Trust's applications, issued a formal statement confirming the commitment of the Pairc Estate (that is to say, PCL, PRL and Barry Lomas personally) to achieving an amicable transfer of the estate to the Trust. But on 3 May 2010 the Trust received information that PCL and PRL had petitioned the Court of Session for judicial review of Scottish Ministers' decision to treat the Trust's Part 3 applications as having been validly made.

The petitions were directed against Scottish Ministers, not against the Trust, since it was the decision of Scottish Ministers that PCL and PRL sought to challenge. However, it is difficult to interpret the objective as being any other than to prevent the Trust's applications proceeding any further by stopping the consultation process, which had already just begun.

PCL and PRL lodged separate petitions because the Trust was seeking to buy the common grazings from PCL and the interposed lease from PRL. However the two petitions were in virtually identical terms, each arguing that Scottish Ministers were wrong in allowing the Trust's applications to proceed to consultation.

There were several grounds on which PCL and PRL challenged the Ministers' decision. Firstly, it was argued that Part 3 of the Land Reform (Scotland) Act 2003 was incompatible with the rights of PCL and PRL under the European Convention on Human Rights and accordingly had been outwith the legislative competence of the Scottish Parliament; and that similarly the Crofting Community Right to Buy (Ballot) (Scotland) Regulations 2004 were outwith the devolved competence of the Scottish Parliament. Put more simply, it was argued that the powers of the Scottish Parliament did not extend to enabling crofting communities compulsorily to acquire land or interests in land belonging to other parties. The Court was asked to annul and, in the meantime, to immediately suspend the operation of Part 3 and the Regulations, to the effect of preventing the buyout going ahead.

Secondly it was argued that Scottish Ministers should have declined to consider the Trust's applications in terms of section 73 (14) of the Land Reform (Scotland) Act 2003, because the applications did not comply with certain of the requirements of section 73, which sets out the circumstances in which a crofting community could competently exercise the right to buy. Ministers, it was argued, should have declared the Trust's applications to be invalid and have rejected them, without embarking on the consultation process.

Thirdly, the Court was asked to find that the ballot authorising the Trust to submit the applications had been flawed in various respects, claiming that it was not secret nor its conduct fair and reasonable. Accordingly the appeal argued that the result of the ballot should be set aside, again with the consequence that the buyout procedure should be halted immediately.

A preliminary hearing of the petitions was held before Lord Matthews on 4 May 2010, to determine whether or not the buyout procedure should be halted there and then, without the need for fuller legal argument on the complicated issues underlying the challenge to Scottish Ministers' decision to proceed with the consultation process.

Lord Matthews refused to order an immediate halt to the buyout procedure, but gave permission to PCL and PRL to appeal his decision and fixed a date of 7 June 2010 for a more detailed consideration of the petitions. In the event neither PCL nor PRL appealed. Instead they postponed the hearing fixed for 7 June 2010 to a date in February 2011. They then cancelled that hearing and agreed that any further hearing on the petitions be postponed indefinitely. The consultation process accordingly went ahead. There never was a judicial review of Ministers' decision to accept the Trust's new Part 3 applications as having been validly made.

COMMENTS ON THE TRUST'S PART 3 APPLICATIONS

Scottish Government received twenty-eight written responses to the Trust's two Part 3 applications. A small number of individuals and organisations responded in support of one or both of the Trust's applications:

- Alasdair Allan MSP;
- Philip McLean, the local elected councillor on CnES;
- Highlands and Islands Enterprise;
- Ravenspoint on behalf of Co-Chomunn na Pairc (a community body run on behalf of the Pairc community);
- Two of the Pairc commons grazing clerks (for Caversta and Habost); and
- Scottish Natural Heritage

A small number of other organisations responded, raising no objections to the applications. These included Historic Scotland.

Surprisingly, no response was submitted by CnES, although there is no doubt that the local authority was a strong supporter of the Trust's two applications. SSE also did not submit a response. In the author's view this is significant given the company's pivotal role in the proposed commercial wind farm. It seems likely if SSE had had any concerns or reservations then it would have objected to the Trust's applications.

Some eleven objections to the applications were submitted by local residents. Most of these were either current or past members of the Pairc Community Council (PCC) or had family connections with them and had been vocal objectors to a commercial wind farm on the estate. It can probably be safely assumed that these objectors were among the eighty-seven people who voted 'no' in the December 2009 ballot.

Although most of the relatively small number of local people who objected to the Part 3 applications had connections with the PCC, there was no objection lodged by the PCC itself. The Trust believed that at one point the PCC was intent on submitting comments opposing the Pairc Trust's applications. Discussions were therefore held between the two organisations. The Trust pointed out that the members of the PCC who opposed the Trust's applications clearly did not represent the views of the vast majority of the local community as indicated by the outcome of the December 2009 ballot which overwhelmingly supported a compulsory buyout using Part 3 of the Act.

The Trust felt it had tried very hard to build bridges with the PCC, particularly in order to explore how the two elected bodies, along with other elected bodies in the area, could best work together in the overall interests of the local community. One example was an invitation from the Trust for the chairman of the PCC to join the Trust's board as an ex officio member. However, this was declined by the PCC.

Scottish Government received six sets of objections representing the interests of Barry Lomas. These came from PCL, PRL, and also Barry Lomas in a personal capacity. They were to each of the two Part 3 applications. In combination, the six responses were long and detailed. In the author's view, they contained a large element of duplication. Barry Lomas's comments in a personal capacity concentrated on the nature of the Pairc Trust, how it dealt with people, and its ability and honesty. In his written submission he described the Trust in terms of 'duplicity, deceit and dishonesty'. He also used the term 'double dealing' in relation to the Trust's twin track strategy – that is, the Trust's approach of exploring possible avenues for an acceptable voluntary transfer whilst at the same time pursuing its Part 3 applications. The Trust took the view that the 2010 Part 3 applications were necessary if it was to achieve the community's wish to purchase the estate – either by effecting a purchase under Part 3 or by bringing about a change in the landlord's willingness to agree reasonable terms under a voluntary transfer.

The Trust characterised the responses from PCL and PRL as being 'pedantic'; 'full of repetitious, false statements'; and 'containing many errors'. A consistent theme of the responses from PCL, PRL and Barry Lomas was that the Trust had failed to follow the legislation or guidance issued by the Scottish Government. This was strongly disputed by the Trust, highlighting the fact that Ministers had accepted its applications as valid as the basis for consultation.

In response to the consultation exercise, the Trust stressed that it believed that its applications were sound and in line with legislation. The few errors of a technical or minor nature in its applications that did come to light were not sufficient, in the Trust's view, to change its overall conclusions that both applications were sound. For example, it emerged that the extensive list of postcode areas and Ordnance Survey one kilometre squares recorded in the application forms contained a few errors. Also, five local residents whose names were on the electoral roll and had therefore received ballot papers were aged under eighteen years at the time of the December 2009 ballot. They should therefore not have been allowed a vote. The Trust requested that Ministers should apply tests of reasonableness and proportionality to any such technical deficiencies in its two applications.

DECISIONS BY MINISTERS ON THE TRUST'S PART 3 APPLICATIONS

There was then a delay while Ministers considered the Trust's applications in the light of all the comments received during the consultation period. Eventually, by letter dated 21 March 2011, the Trust received news that Scottish Ministers had approved both its 2010 Part 3 applications, the first time such approval had ever been granted. It should be noted that the date of the letter was just before the period of purdah prior to the Scottish Parliamentary elections in May 2011 during which Ministers would have been unable to make announcements (such as this decision) which could be regarded as having political implications. Given the complexity and pioneering nature of the applications and the statutory consultation period, this was perhaps not an unreasonable time frame within which to reach a decision – although it was a little over one year from the date of submission of the applications, and nearly seven months from the closing date for the receipt of the Trust's response to consultation comments. Simultaneously (by letter of 21 March 2011), Scottish Ministers rejected the Trust's 2005 Part 3 application.

The three decision letters are significant and of wide ranging interest collectively and each in its own right. They are, therefore, reproduced as appendices in Appendix One. Each is of particular relevance and interest to other crofting communities who might consider submitting any future Part 3 Consent to Buy Eligible Croft Land etc applications – of which, to date, there have been none. For the two successful 2010 Part 3 applications, large parts of the text of both approval letters are (unsurprisingly) the same. However, due to the differing nature of the two applications there are some variations in the texts of the approval letters – which are worth studying.

The rejection of the 2005 application came as no surprise to the Trust. Two key reasons were cited by Scottish Ministers for rejecting the Trust's proposals. First, they were not satisfied the Trust's proposals were compatible with furthering the achievement of sustainable development. And, second, they were not satisfied that it was in the public interest that the Trust's right to buy should be exercised.

In terms of not meeting the sustainable development test, Ministers criticised, inter alia, the Trust's 2005 Business Plan as being too generalised, lacking in detail and not providing any clear benefit for the local community. Neither did the plan (in Ministers' views) show how ownership of the common grazings would make a real difference to the community – particularly due to the limited income generating opportunities outlined.

In terms of not meeting the public interest test Ministers stated that the Trust had not provided any clear evidence of how the acquisition of the common grazings would provide benefits in the short, medium or long term to the community. Ministers also stated that, in effect, the 2005 application had been superseded by the Trust's 2010 applications.

The Trust regarded the two 2010 applications as superseding its 2005 application. The author's view is that the 2010 applications were altogether stronger, more detailed, more thorough and more robust than the 2005 application. This is hardly surprising given the passage of time and the lessons learnt by the Trust from its 2005 application. The 2005 application did not have the benefit of including the interposed lease – without which the Trust acknowledged that it would not have had adequate powers to achieve sustainable development.

Of course, the 2005 application could not have included the interposed lease. At that time the Trust thought that it was applying for consent to buy the common grazings without the burden of the interposed lease. Its consequences, as determined by the Land Court, only became apparent later. Even if the consequences had been known in 2005, it would not then have been competent in law to buy the interest in the interposed lease. That only became possible after the Scottish Parliament's amendment of the 2003 Act.

CHAPTER SIX: SUMMARY AND REFLECTIONS

The success of the 2010 Part 3 applications in gaining Ministerial approval in March 2011 can be seen in retrospect as a key turning point in the Pairc Estate community buyout. It was a huge step forward for the Trust, after all its work in preparing the applications and dealing with the volume of comments and objections from the landlord. It was also widely seen as a landmark decision by the Government, the first ever approval of an application by a crofting community body under Part 3 of the Act.

In the author's opinion, it would have been quite odd if Scottish Ministers had not given consent for the buyout to go ahead although doubtless there had been lengthy consideration of the legal and other risks involved in an untested area of policy. Giving crofting communities the right to buy the land they occupied was an

important plank in Ministers' land reform policy which had been
formulated to deal with circumstances like those which prevailed
in Pairc.

As events transpired (see chapter seven and following chapters),
the decision did not immediately lead to the Trust taking ownership
of the estate. It actually took more than a further four and a
half years. Nor was the eventual purchase achieved through the
Part 3 route. But, from the time of the Ministerial approvals, the
landlord was, in the author's view, probably fighting somewhat
of a rearguard action. Once the first part of his appeal against
the Ministerial decisions was rejected by the Court of Session, it
appears to the author that he probably gradually came to regard a
community buyout as inevitable.

- CHAPTER SEVEN -

A Breakthrough at Last

PREPARING FOR A VALUATION

Once Scottish Ministers had approved the Trust's two 2010 Part 3 applications in March 2011, the next stage in the buyout procedure, as set out in the Act, was to determine the price which the Trust would have to pay for the land and the interposed lease. That involved the appointment by Ministers, within seven days of their consent being granted, of an independent valuer to carry out a valuation. A firm of chartered surveyors, DMH Baird Lumsden, was appointed to carry out that task, which was to be completed within a maximum period of six weeks. When the valuer's report was received, the Trust would have a period of twenty-one days to consider whether or not it wished to go ahead with the buyout at the price fixed by the valuation.

The aim of the valuation exercise was to ensure that the landowner received and the Trust paid a fair price (the market value) for the land and interposed lease. The Trust should not be allowed to purchase cheaply or at a financial loss to the landlord, but nor should the landowner be allowed to charge a price in excess of what he might reasonably have expected to receive if the land and interposed lease had been put up for sale on the open market. The definition of market value is set out more fully in Section 88(6) of the 2003 Act.

The purpose of the valuation process (as set out in Scottish Government guidance of June 2009 on the right to buy under Part 3 of the Act) was to determine:

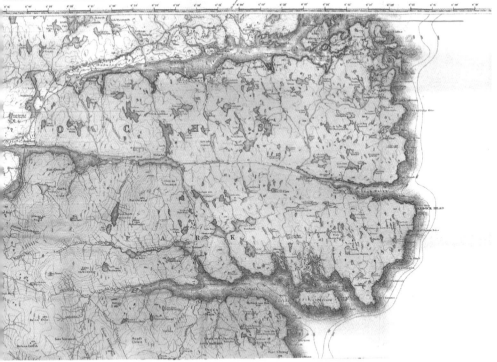

Plate 1. Map of Pairc Estate from the title deed of sale by Lord Leverhulme to Pairc Crofters Ltd in 1924 (Register of Sasines)

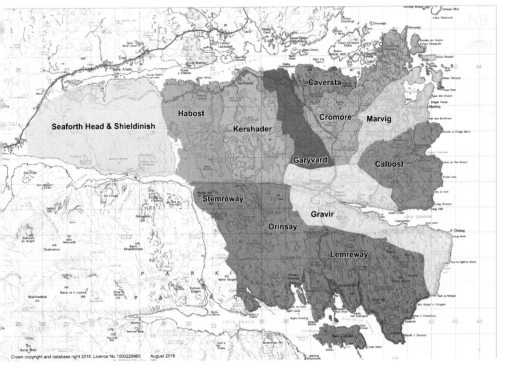

Plate 2. Map showing the approximate boundaries of Steimreway and the crofting townships of Pairc (courtesy of Comhairle nan Eilean Siar)

Plate 3. Ruins of the former village of Steimreway (courtesy of John Randall)

Plate 4. View of the village of Calbost from the south (courtesy of John Randall)

Plate 5. View of the village of Lemreway in 2006 showing hay harvested in the traditional way (courtesy of John Randall)

Plate 6. Members of the wider Pairc community at the deserted village of Steimreway in 2010 (courtesy of Donnie Morrison)

Plate 7. Residents of Pairc queuing to vote in the first community ballot in November 2004 (courtesy Donnie Morrison)

Plate 8. Officials of Comhairle nan Eilean Siar counting the vote following the third community ballot in May 2014 (courtesy Donnie Morrison)

Plate 9. Members of Pairc Trust at a public meeting in March 2011 (courtesy of Donnie Morrison)

Plate 10. Directors of Pairc Trust in June 2005 with Sandra Holmes of HIE (second left) (courtesy of Donnie Morrison)

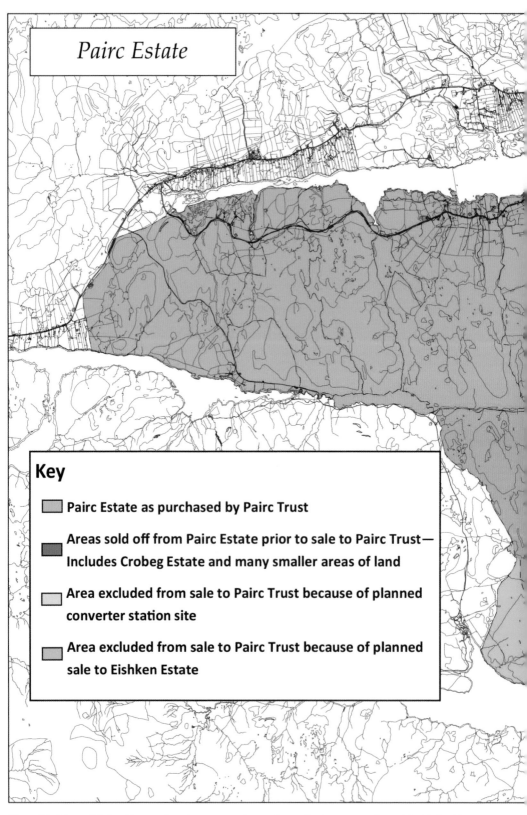

Key

Pairc Estate as purchased by Pairc Trust

Areas sold off from Pairc Estate prior to sale to Pairc Trust—Includes Crobeg Estate and many smaller areas of land

Area excluded from sale to Pairc Trust because of planned converter station site

Area excluded from sale to Pairc Trust because of planned sale to Eishken Estate

Plate 11. Map of Pairc Estate showing approximate boundaries as purchased by Pairc Trust in December 2015 (updated and adapted from map prepared by Registers of Scotland for Pairc Trust dated September 2014)

Plate 12. Alasdair Allan MSP and Angus McDowall in July 2016 unveiling the plaque to mark the completion of the buyout (courtesy of Donnie Morrison)

Plate 13. David Cameron of Harris beside the plaque at Kershader in July 2016 (courtesy of Donnie Morrison)

Plate 14. Crowd outside Ravenspoint at the celebratory event in July 2016 (courtesy of Donnie Morrison)

Plate 15. Young members of the Pairc community dancing at the celebratory event in July 2016 (courtesy of Donnie Morrison)

Plate 16. Kristine Kennedy, Royal National Mòd go medal winner from Orinsay, singing at the celebra event in July 2016 (courtesy of Donnie Morrison)

- The open market value of the sale as if it were between a willing seller and a willing buyer;
- Compensation for any depreciation in the value of other land, tenants' interests and other interests belonging to the seller as a result of a forced sale; and
- Compensation for any disturbance to the seller resulting from a forced sale.

The guidance is also clear on the role of the independent valuer – being that of an expert but not of an arbiter. The relevance of that distinction is that the valuer in assessing the value of the land and interposed lease, was to rely on her/his own expertise in valuing land and not simply on evidence from the landowner and Trust supporting their views on what the appropriate values should be. Both parties were entitled to make their views known to the valuer, but her/his job was not to decide which of the parties' inevitably opposing views was preferable. Instead, she/he was there to determine the value of the land and lease by applying her/his own knowledge of the market, albeit after taking into account what both parties had to say.

In such a valuation exercise, the price fixed by the valuer is the expression of her/his opinion as to what price would have been achieved if there had been an open market sale. If either the landowner or the Trust were to disagree with the opinion of the valuer, the legislation gives either party the right to challenge that opinion by appealing to the Scottish Land Court. The Land Court could then either uphold the valuer's opinion or could reassess the value of the land and interposed lease, substituting its own assessment of value for that determined by the valuer.

However, all the intricacies of the valuation exercise were to be of academic interest only. Gordon King, the partner in DMH Baird Lumsden who was to carry out the valuation, had only just made contact with the landowner and the Trust to clarify certain aspects of his instructions from Scottish Ministers, when PCL and PRL in April 2011 submitted appeals (under section 91(1) of the 2003 Act) against Scottish Ministers' decision to grant the Trust's applications for consent to exercise the right to buy.

THE LANDLORD'S APPEAL AGAINST THE DECISION OF SCOTTISH GOVERNMENT TO APPROVE THE TRUST'S 2010 PART 3 APPLICATIONS

The appeals were lodged in the Sheriff Court in Stornoway, as the legislation provided that the Sheriff of the Sheriffdom in which the subject of the buyout lay, was to have jurisdiction to hear the appeals. Legally, these appeals by PCL and PRL were quite distinct from the earlier petitions which PCL and PRL had made to the Court of Session for judicial review of Scottish Ministers' decision to treat the Trust's applications for consent to the proposed buyout as having been validly made. Although these petitions had been lodged in March 2010, PCL and PRL had not taken them forward, after Lord Matthews had refused to suspend the consultation process, at the preliminary hearing on 4 May 2010.

Although the appeals to the Sheriff involved a challenge to a different decision of Scottish Ministers to that challenged by the petitions for judicial review in the Court of Session, the grounds on which the challenge was made were largely the same. In particular the power of the Scottish Parliament to have enacted Part 3 of the 2003 Act allowing crofting communities to buy their croft land and the Buyout Ballot Regulations of 2004 were again challenged. As these challenges raised issues with regard to the European Convention on Human Rights, in respect of which the Court of Session had exclusive jurisdiction, the Sheriff referred those aspects of the appeals to the Court of Session, to be dealt with before the other aspects of the appeals which the Sheriff could competently deal with.

That referral was made in October 2011, but it was not until July 2012 that three judges of the Inner House of the Court of Session heard the legal debate on the European Convention of Human Rights (ECHR) and devolution issues between senior counsel instructed by PCL and PRL and by Scottish Ministers. Although the case was in relation to the Trust's right to buy, the Trust did not take part in the legal debate, believing that any arguments which it might have wanted to make in support of upholding the Ministers' decision would in any event be made by counsel for the Ministers. There would have been little or no benefit derived by the Trust from incurring what would have been the substantial expense of being represented at the hearing.

In December 2012 the three judges, chaired by the Lord President, Lord Gill, who had a particular interest in rural matters including expertise in crofting law, issued their judgements. They unanimously rejected the arguments put forward on behalf of PCL and PRL. This again was seen as a landmark judgement, of wide interest not only in Pairc but to those in Scotland interested in land reform and indeed more widely.

Only once the Court of Session had made its judgement, would the case have been due to be referred back to the Sheriff Court to consider the other aspects of the appeal. Pending the decision on the ECHR and devolution issues, the appeal procedure in the Sheriff Court was suspended ('sisted'). However, before the Court of Session decision had been issued, discussions had resumed in earnest between Barry Lomas and the Trust in relation to an amicable transfer of the whole of the Pairc Estate. Therefore, once the Court of Session made its decision, PCL and PRL and Ministers agreed that the 'sist' in the Sheriff Court should not be recalled, in order to enable those discussions to continue unaffected by the legislative timetable for the Part 3 buyout.

RESUMPTION OF NEGOTIATIONS FOR A VOLUNTARY TRANSFER

As outlined in earlier chapters, discussions with the landlord about a possible voluntary transfer (sometimes referred to as an amicable transfer) of the estate had taken place from time to time at several different points since the start of the buyout. Such discussions had taken place in the early years prior to the Trust's first ballot in November 2004 under Part 3 of the Act. The possibility of a voluntary estate transfer was raised again at a meeting called by Barry Lomas immediately following the Land Court hearing to determine the validity of the interposed lease on 13 June 2007. There followed several inconclusive attempts to agree how such a voluntary estate transfer might be achieved (see chapter five).

The support which Barry Lomas expressed for an amicable transfer of the whole of the Pairc Estate contrasts with what appeared to be his determination to oppose the Trust's applications for consent to exercise the right to buy the common grazings and interposed lease under Part 3 of the 2003 Act. It may have been the anticipated determination of the community to pursue the acquisition of the land they occupied which had prompted him to create the interposed lease in the first place and then to defend his position by petitioning for judicial review of Ministers' acceptance of the Part 3 applications as valid and then appealing against Ministers' decision to consent to those applications. But without his input this can only be speculation.

A further round of discussions about a possible voluntary transfer of the estate had got underway in late 2011, and these were given fresh impetus by the Court of Session's judgements in December 2012 against the landlord's appeal. The chequered history of previous discussions led to a suggestion that it might assist in bringing the latest attempt to a successful outcome if an independent mediator could be found. David Cameron, a Harris resident, agreed to take on this role as a mutually trusted individual. David is a Harris businessman with a great commitment to community development. He was also the founding Chair of Community Land Scotland (CLS), the umbrella organisation established in 2010 to bring together actual and aspiring community landowners to exchange experience on good practice and promote the case for community land ownership. He had been a key figure in the community buyout of the 55,000 acre North Harris Estate in 2003.

David Cameron and his family knew Barry Lomas and his family well. He also knew several of the Pairc Trust directors. Interestingly, the author has been told that both Barry Lomas and the Pairc Trust approached David Cameron independently to enquire if he would mediate in discussions regarding the transfer of the Pairc Estate. The approach by the Pairc Trust was made in March 2013 and by a representative of Barry Lomas a year earlier. David therefore had the confidence of both sides. He began his role in March 2013 and finished in mid April 2014.

It is important to state that David Cameron undertook this role purely in a personal capacity, not linked to his chairmanship of CLS, though the organisation was content for him to do this. Also, David received no payment for his services, despite spending, on average, between six and twelve hours per week on this. He had separate meetings with Barry Lomas, the Pairc Trust, and the lawyers for both sides, and also chaired meetings at which Barry Lomas and representatives of the Pairc Trust were present together. In terms of the Pairc Trust, David Cameron had meetings with:

- The chairman on his own;
- The Pairc Trust's three office bearers – Angus McDowall (chairman from 2009 and a director since the Trust was formed), John Randall (vice chairman from 2009 and a director since November 2008), and Maretta Campbell (secretary and treasurer, and a director since November 2011); and
- The Trust as a whole. David took the majority view on substantive matters if there was any significant difference of opinion amongst directors.

Lawyers were not present at most meetings. Instead, if legal issues were raised, both parties would speak separately to their lawyers.

David made it clear to both parties from the outset that his role was to listen and mediate between them, and not to negotiate on matters. He also reserved the right to walk away at any time if he felt that progress had been unduly stalled or had reached deadlock. His initial analysis was that both parties had boxed themselves into positions from which they felt it was difficult to move. His tactic to begin with was not to try to get the two parties to speak to one another face to face but for him to go back and forth to establish common ground if there was any to be found. Essentially, this initially revolved around establishing if the estate was for sale and if so at what price; and from there to try to find any common ground between the two parties on a mutually acceptable sale price and conditions of sale.

In the author's opinion both the Pairc Trust and Barry Lomas owe David Cameron a great debt of gratitude for mediating the eventual successful voluntary transfer of the Pairc Estate. His input was critical and without it there could well have been either an unsuccessful outcome to the voluntary transfer discussions or the matter would have carried on for far longer.

There were a number of factors leading to the ramping up of discussions between the landlord and the Trust in 2013 about a voluntary transfer of the estate. The Court of Session's comprehensive rejection in December 2012 of Barry Lomas's arguments about human rights in relation to the Part 3 applications was probably one such pivotal event.

Also, approval of the commercial wind farm was by this time becoming to appear increasingly unlikely. The prospect of a large scale commercial wind farm on the Pairc Estate – which had seemed a real possibility in 2008 and 2009 – had gradually faded. A revised application for a reduced scheme of twenty-six turbines with a total generating capacity of 94MW annually over twenty-five years had been submitted by SSE to Scottish Ministers in February 2009. But it became clear that a quick decision would not be taken even on this reduced scheme. There were, inter alia, serious issues relating to the impact of the proposal on Golden Eagles and White-tailed Sea Eagles which required further lengthy bird surveys and evaluation.

The interaction between the wind farm proposal and the Pairc community buyout may also have been a complicating factor at a political level although that can only be conjecture on the part of the author. Scottish Ministers were of course generally sympathetic to and supportive of the Pairc community buyout initiative as this would have furthered the political objective, embodied in the legislation, of transferring more land to the ownership of local crofting communities. Ministers, therefore, might not have been in a hurry to take decisions about a commercial wind farm which, in turn, would have increased the value (and thus the selling price) of the estate. It may well be, also, that similar considerations led to CnES not putting pressure on Ministers for a decision on the wind farm. But, again, that can only be speculation on the part of the author.

Finally, it became clear that without a positive decision on an interconnector cable (subject to continual delays and escalating costs) with greatly increased capacity between the Western Isles and the mainland, a large development such as the SSE wind farm for Pairc could not proceed even if Government approval was given to the scheme. The net result was that SSE seemed gradually to have lost interest in the Pairc wind farm scheme over time, although it did not formally withdraw from the lease with PRL until September 2014.

It could have been that, following the Court of Session's decision, Barry Lomas came to realise that a buyout was inevitable. He seems from that point to have decided he should negotiate seriously with the Trust in order to obtain the best possible terms from his perspective from a community buyout. The escalating cost of mounting legal appeals was perhaps also a factor.

The landlord's aim may have been not only to maximise the price which the Pairc Trust would have to pay to purchase the whole estate and interposed lease but also to recoup the legal and other costs which he claimed had been incurred in dealing with the Trust's Part 3 applications and in finalising a voluntary transfer. The very large compensation claims which he submitted to the Trust and the Scottish Government for dealing with the 2005 and 2010 Part 3 applications are discussed in subsequent chapters.

The complex discussions mediated by David Cameron between the Trust and Barry Lomas eventually led to an agreement in autumn 2013 on a non legally binding set of Heads of Terms which would allow for a voluntary transfer of the whole estate. These are covered in detail in chapter eight. The possibility of the Trust continuing to pursue the remaining legal stages to take forward the two Part 3 applications still of course remained an option.

FUND RAISING

Meanwhile, the Pairc Trust had embarked on a public fund raising campaign to help it to be in a better position to purchase the estate, whether this was achieved via the Part 3 route or through a voluntary agreement with Barry Lomas. The 2003 Act specifies (Section 87(2)) that a CCB – such as the Pairc Trust – must pay for the land (and, also in this case, the interposed lease) within six months from the date on which Ministers consent to a Part 3 application.

This meant that, in normal circumstances, the Trust would have had to complete the purchase before the end of September 2011. The Trust had therefore established a local and national funding appeal in the spring of 2011 in the expectation that, following the valuation commissioned by the Government, the Pairc Trust would need to raise financial resources to complete a funding package to purchase the estate and also to take forward the first projects under its business plan. Even though the independent valuation was halted as a result of Barry Lomas's appeal, the Trust continued with its community buyout fund appeal. It pledged that all donations would be acknowledged and kept in a separate fund to be used only for the purchase of the land and lease, and to fund initial developments after the buyout. In the event of the buyout not proceeding, all contributions would be returned where details of the donor were available. The initial target for the fund was £150,000.

CHAPTER SEVEN: SUMMARY AND REFLECTIONS

This chapter has outlined developments over the period from March 2011 (when Scottish Ministers approved the Trust's two 2010 Part 3 applications) through to Autumn 2013 (by which time the landlord had entered into a non legally binding Heads of Terms agreement with the Trust for the voluntary transfer of the whole estate). This important change in the landlord's position was due in the author's view to two main factors:

- First, the initial part of the landlord's appeal against Scottish Ministers' approval of the 2010 Part 3 applications (regarding ECHR and devolution arguments) was comprehensively rejected by the Court of Session in December 2012. While it was still possible that the Sheriff Court in Stornoway would uphold the other parts of the landlord's appeal, it may have seemed to Barry Lomas that there was now a real prospect of the Trust being able to see through to a successful conclusion its Part 3 approach – resulting in the landlord being forced to sell the common grazings at a price determined by an independent valuation.

- Second, and linked to the first factor, the prospect of the value of the estate being greatly increased by the approval and implementation of the SSE commercial wind farm proposal had faded.

- The combination of these two key factors could have led to Barry Lomas concluding that a community buyout was becoming much more inevitable; and that, in his own best financial interests, he should explore a negotiated settlement with the Trust for a voluntary transfer of the estate. This held out the possibility of him receiving a higher price for the sale of the estate than was likely under a Part 3 sale, together with substantial compensation claims.

From the Trust's viewpoint, a crucial breakthrough had been achieved in that the landlord was now prepared to agree to a deal for a voluntary transfer which, in the view of the majority of its board, was capable of being recommended to the community. The complex details of this negotiated option (together with its advantages and disadvantages compared with pursuing the Part 3 route; and how it was considered and approved by the community and eventually implemented in a legally binding form) are discussed and described in the following chapter.

- CHAPTER EIGHT -
Completing a
Voluntary Transfer

It took the Trust much of 2013 to negotiate the principles of an acceptable voluntary transfer deal which it felt could be considered and judged by the local community alongside the alternative option of continuing to pursue the Part 3 approach with a view to purchasing most (though not all) of the estate through the procedures set out in the legislation. Discussions during that period were mediated by David Cameron, and also included negotiations on a number of related matters with Nick Oppenheim, owner of the neighbouring Eishken Estate. By November 2013 discussions had progressed to the stage of a draft non-binding Heads of Terms being agreed between the Pairc Trust and Barry Lomas for a voluntary transfer of the estate and the interposed lease, subject to endorsement by the community.

NEGOTIATING THE TERMS OF A VOLUNTARY TRANSFER OPTION

The late summer and autumn of 2013 was the crucial period when Pairc Trust directors considered whether to recommend to the community that a voluntary purchase of the estate should be pursued on the basis of the non-binding Heads of Terms agreement negotiated with Barry Lomas or whether the Trust should seek to see its 2010 Part 3 applications through to a successful conclusion. In effect, this was decision time as to which of the 'twin tracks' should be selected as the preferred mechanism for achieving the community buyout. In practice, however, both tracks were retained as possible mechanisms for acquiring the estate until one of them had succeeded. For example, if the voluntary route was chosen and subsequently proved to be unsuccessful, there was nothing preventing the Trust, at such a point, reverting to the Part 3 route.

The key elements of the draft non-binding Heads of Terms for a voluntary transfer were:

- The Pairc Trust on behalf of the community would buy all of the land (including the in bye land, most of the Steimreway grazings, and the foreshore – if the Crown Estate confirmed it had no interest in this) with the exception of: (a) the prospective Gravir Converter Station site of approximately 52 acres (21 hectares) the sale of which was at the time being negotiated by PCL with SSE and Scottish Hydro Electric Transmission Limited (SHETL) – a company in the SSE group which was responsible for building the interconnector cable to link in with the then planned route of the cable between Lewis and the Scottish mainland; and (b) an area near Beinn Eishken on south Steimreway amounting to approximately 435 acres (175 hectares) which would be purchased under a separate arrangement altogether by Nick Oppenheim, the owner of the Eishken Estate.
- The Pairc Trust would also take over the interests of: (a) PCL and PRL in the interposed lease; (b) PRL in the sub lease between PRL and SSE; and (c) PCL in the interposed lease between PCL and Pairc Agricultural Ltd (also controlled by Barry Lomas) which covered the Steimreway grazings area. This meant the Trust would stand to benefit under the terms of the sub lease between PRL and SSE from a substantial income if the SSE wind farm proposal became operational. At this point in time the Trust understood that SSE had transferred its interest in the sub lease to a company owned by Nick Oppenheim. This would not have affected the income which would be due to the Pairc Trust should SSE's wind farm proposal (still under consideration by Scottish Ministers) have proceeded. In fact this transfer did not take place, and SSE withdrew from the sub lease in September 2014.
- Notwithstanding the above, Barry Lomas would still benefit from any commercial wind farm which went ahead on the Pairc Estate following purchase of the land by the

community. He would not benefit from any community wind farm as defined in the agreement. This arrangement was unusual and it may seem illogical that Barry Lomas should be paid for the value of the interposed lease and, in addition, derive income if a commercial wind farm went ahead after a transfer of ownership. In principle, the value of the interposed lease (whereby the Pairc Trust purchased the rights of PRL) should have already included an estimate of the stream of income which PRL stood to gain from a wind farm development at the time of the sale. In effect, it appears that Barry Lomas would be paid twice if a commercial wind farm became operational. However, without such an agreement for future income from a commercial wind farm, it was clear to the Trust that Barry Lomas would not have agreed to a voluntary transfer of the land and leases.

Even if Barry Lomas benefited by receiving income from any future commercial wind farm development in terms of the sub lease to SSE, this would not have been at the expense of the Trust. It would also benefit from any further commercial wind farm development to the same extent. This arrangement was only possible because of separate negotiations between the Trust and Nick Oppenheim. He is a successful businessman who has owned the Eishken Estate since 1989. He has also been a generous local benefactor, having given substantial financial and other support over a number of years to a wide variety of community projects in Pairc. Moreover, he was successful in obtaining consent from Scottish Ministers for a major wind farm on part of the Eishken Estate. At one point he was contemplating taking over SSE's interests in a commercial wind farm on the Pairc Estate on the basis of guaranteeing that, if a commercial wind farm on the Pairc Estate proceeded after the sale of the Estate to the Trust, Barry Lomas would also receive the same income from it as the Trust would derive. However, the draft Heads of Terms agreement also stipulated that Barry Lomas's interests in such a wind farm development would expire after the first twenty-five years of electricity generation. Thereafter, if the wind farm continued (or was replaced) all future rental income would then accrue solely to the Pairc community. The Trust also negotiated a clause to restrict the number of turbines to a maximum of twenty-six (unless the Pairc community decided that it wished to see additional turbines consented).

- The combined purchase price of the land and leases would be £500,000. This was much higher than the most recent independent valuation of £300,000 (£130,000 value for the land; and £170,000 value for the leases based on the hope value of a commercial wind farm at the time of the valuation). However, it was also well below Barry Lomas's initial request of £1million for a voluntary sale.

Despite the discrepancy of £200,000 between the proposed purchase price and the independent valuation, the Pairc Trust was confident that the £500,000 purchase price could be 100 per cent funded by a combination of money from the Scottish Land Fund (SLF), HIE, CnES, and its own resources. The latter included money raised from the local community and others as part of a fund raising campaign started in 2011, and a large sum received from Eishken Nominees Limited (one of Nick Oppenheim's companies and the company which owns the Eishken Estate) for an access agreement over the Eishken road – see below. Discussions had already taken place with the funding bodies. In addition, the Pairc Trust expected that SLF and HIE would provide revenue funding to employ two members of staff for the first two years following community ownership. And, it anticipated that the SLF would provide a further £50,000 to cover legal costs.

Nick Oppenheim indirectly played a crucial role in helping the Pairc Trust achieve a voluntary buyout through his company Eishken Nominees Limited. This gave both Barry Lomas (whilst still owner of the Pairc Estate) and the Pairc Trust (the then prospective owner) £300,000 each (plus £5,000 to the Trust for legal costs) under the terms of legal contracts giving the Eishken wind farm developers right of access over a widened Eishken road (which runs within the Pairc Estate for over three miles) in connection with the already consented large scale commercial wind farm on the Eishken Estate and any others that might follow.

Having a guaranteed access for the intended wind farms was critical for the developers and investors involved in the Eishken schemes. This almost certainly explains the financial arrangement reached with the Pairc Trust. Although the Trust did not own the estate at the time, the financial arrangement was probably felt necessary by the wind farm developers and investors to ensure that whatever happened in relation to the buyout there would be an enforceable contract in place whoever owned the Pairc Estate at the relevant time. If Barry Lomas alone had undertaken to grant the necessary access rights, that obligation would not necessarily have been transferred to the Trust. There would have been even greater uncertainty for the developers and investors on this issue if the buyout had been achieved under Part 3. The legal agreement with the Trust therefore gave the developers guaranteed certainty on access.

At the time of writing, the Muaitheabhal commercial wind farm had received consent (from Scottish Ministers in January 2010) for thirty-three turbines each 145 metres in height (to the blade tip) and of 3.6 megawatts output (totalling 118.8 megawatts). The original application was submitted on behalf of Beinn Mhor Power and Crionaig Power Ltd in 2004 for 133 turbines with a total output of 399 megawatts. A revised application was submitted in 2006 for 53 turbines with an output of 159 megawatts. This was further reduced to a proposal of 39 turbines (with a total output of 140.4 megawatts) into which a public inquiry was held in 2008. Scottish Government's decision letter of January 2010 for determination of the 39 turbines scheme consented 33 of the 39 turbines.

In December 2010 an application on behalf of Crionaig Power Ltd was submitted to Scottish Government for an extension to the Muaitheabhal scheme (east of the consented area) comprising 6 turbines each of 3.6 megawatts and 150 metres height to blade tip (with a total output of 21.6 megawatts). Ministers gave consent to this extension in December 2011 (without a local public inquiry). However, neither of the consented schemes has been constructed at the time of writing; nor could they become operational until an interconnector to the Scottish mainland is in place.

Following the access agreement, Nick Oppenheim sold the rights of the Muaitheabhal wind farm to another company, so realising the value of the development and, amongst other things, allowing very significant amounts of cash to be released to the Muaitheabhal Community Wind Farm Trust (MCWFT) to start its operations – despite the wind farm not having been constructed. The MCWFT is, as its name suggests, a community wind farm trust. It was established in 2012 with the purpose of distributing the community benefit funds available from the wind farm development – its priority areas being Pairc, Kinloch, and the settlements along Loch Seaforth in north Harris.

The Pairc Trust treated the £300,000 it received from Eishken Nominees Ltd for the right of access over the Eishken Road as a donation – although, unlike other contributions made to the fund raising campaign, the Trust was free to use the money for purposes other than purchase of the estate. It was to prove crucial to the Trust's ability to raise the funds for the eventual voluntary transfer of the estate.

DECIDING BETWEEN THE VOLUNTARY TRANSFER OPTION OR CONTINUING WITH PART 3

After full debate and discussion within the board of the Trust, a clear majority of directors concluded that the voluntary transfer approach on the terms negotiated should be recommended to the community. However, that view was not unanimous. According to information from the Trust to the author, one director in particular was critical of how the office bearers had negotiated the draft terms with Barry Lomas and strongly disagreed with the decision not to recommend continuing to pursue the Part 3 option at this point after so much effort had been put into it. He was unhappy that a voluntary agreement would result in a purchase price being paid for the land and lease which was well above any of the independent valuations that had been undertaken at various points of the process – and considerably in excess of what a Part 3 route, if successful, was likely to produce (though a Part 3 route would not include any of the in bye land, or the Steimreway grazings).

The advantages and disadvantages of the two alternative options were put to a public meeting of the Trust on 21 November 2013. The Trust set out what it saw as the advantages and disadvantages of the two options.

The key advantage of the voluntary transfer option was that the community would acquire the whole estate including the in bye land and most of the Steimreway grazings. This would avoid the difficulty with the Part 3 option of having an indeterminate period when crofters would have two landlords; and the need to return to Barry Lomas in due course to see whether or not he would be prepared to negotiate the sale of the rest of the estate – or, alternatively, of having to submit a further Part 3 application to acquire it. The voluntary option also seemed at the time a quicker and more certain route to acquiring the whole estate, though in the event, it took much longer than anticipated. However, it is not known how long the alternative Part 3 route would have taken to conclude in comparison. For example, there was no certainty over when the Sheriff Court would have met to consider the second part of Barry Lomas's appeal. Moreover, there was no certainty that the Sheriff would have dismissed it.

Although the Pairc Trust believed there were strong arguments of proportionality, it knew that its 2010 Part 3 applications contained some minor errors. It was possible, therefore, that a Sheriff Court could uphold the landlord's appeal on technical grounds. There was no right of appeal in such an event, the Sheriff's decision being final. That then would have been the end in the immediate future of the community's aspirations to own the estate's common grazings through the Part 3 mechanism. The uncertainty was further compounded by the Pairc Estate being a test case – the Part 3 route never having been taken through to successful conclusion before (or since, at the time of writing).

While the price the Trust would pay for the estate under the voluntary option (£500,000) was almost certainly well above what the Part 3 valuation would be, the Trust knew that it could raise this money from its own resources and commitments or advanced discussions with funding bodies.

The advantages and disadvantages of the Part 3 option were virtually the mirror image of the voluntary option. The key elements of the Part 3 option were:

- It only encompassed the estate's common grazings, not the whole estate. Therefore, until the remainder of the estate was purchased (by whatever route) this option would not include the Steimreway agricultural grazings (where a significant element of the SSE wind farm proposal was located) or the in bye land. It could also not avoid the complication of the Pairc crofters having two different landlords for an unspecified period.

- If successful, it represented a potentially much cheaper option than a voluntary transfer. The most recent independent valuation of £300,000 (for the land and the leases) was for the whole estate. Therefore, for a Part 3 application (covering only the common grazings which account for approximately 75 per cent of the estate) the valuation was likely to be lower. However, the Trust always had an aspiration to own the entire estate, which would incur an additional cost over and above the 2010 Part 3 applications, no matter how the rest of the estate was acquired (either through a voluntary transfer or a further Part 3 application). While the likely purchase price was lower, the Trust could afford the higher price of the voluntary option.

- Under a successful Part 3 purchase, the Pairc Trust would receive the entire rental from the turbines of any wind farm located on the common grazings area of the estate and Barry Lomas would receive nothing. The proposed SSE wind farm had fourteen of its twenty-six turbines situated on the common grazings (the others being on the Steimreway grazings). The likely annual income available to the Trust from the fourteen turbines, if the development ever went ahead, was likely to be in the order of £181,000, amounting to approximately £4.5 million over twenty-five years. However, as already noted, the prospect for the wind farm had faded considerably.

- The end result of a Part 3 option was uncertain and the timescale unclear. The timetable for getting the landlord's appeal back into the Stornoway Sheriff Court was unknown and beyond the Pairc Trust's control and influence. There was no guarantee that the Sheriff, whose decision was final, would reject the landlord's appeal. Furthermore, even if the Sheriff did reject the appeal, the landlord would still have the right to appeal an independent valuation of the land and lease to the Scottish Land Court. The timetable for this was unknown. After the landlord had exhausted the appeal process, the SLC could confirm a final valuation which was higher or lower than that of an independent valuer.

- Finally, it was known that some people in the local Pairc community preferred a voluntary approach in principle

since it did not force the landlord to sell against his will –
despite legislation being in place to allow for a forced sale
when a landlord was not prepared to sell voluntarily.

After questions and discussion, those present at the public meeting
overwhelmingly endorsed the voluntary transfer approach by
a show of hands – 56 in favour, 0 against, and 4 abstentions.
However, it was agreed that the matter should be the subject of a
further (secret) ballot once the voluntary agreement had been put
in the form of a draft offer for the estate which could then be made
available for inspection by those in the community eligible to vote.

In the light of the outcome of the public meeting, lawyers acting
for the Pairc Trust and Barry Lomas therefore proceeded to prepare
a draft offer for the estate and leases based on the non-binding
Heads of Terms. This new draft offer was a document of over twenty
pages of detailed and often complex legal conditions. It was made
available for public inspection in the Pairc area prior to the further
postal ballot of the community.

The community approved the voluntary transfer option in a further
postal ballot, the result of which was announced on 1 May 2014.
The question posed was:

Do you agree to the amicable estate transfer of the Pairc Estate
to Pairc Trust on behalf of the Pairc Community on the terms
negotiated between Pairc Trust and Pairc Estate?

The ballot was not a statutory one, though it was again conducted
for the Trust by CnES. It had originally been intended to hold the
ballot for the votes to be counted on 13 March 2014. However, this
had to be cancelled by the Pairc Trust since it had not been possible
to finalise the detailed documentation in the draft offer document
in time for the ballot. The main reason for this was that, according
to the Pairc Trust, Barry Lomas tried to amend the agreement so
that he would receive income from any commercial wind farm
beyond the agreed initial twenty-five year period – to which the
Trust refused to agree. The Trust cancelled the March ballot and
Barry Lomas did not pursue that option any further. This was, in the
author's view, a significant episode since it demonstrated that the
Trust was not prepared to depart from the Heads of Terms already
agreed by the board of the Pairc Trust. Had Barry Lomas not moved

on this matter it is very likely that the Trust would have seriously considered changing course and pursuing its Part 3 applications.

The result of the postal ballot was that 166 voted in favour of a voluntary transfer of the estate on the terms negotiated by the Trust; and 77 voted against. That meant that 68 per cent of those who voted (on a turnout of 62.7 per cent) were in favour of a voluntary transfer – an almost identical level of support for the motion voted on in December 2009, thus demonstrating a holding up of local support during that period for community ownership

DRAWING UP A LEGALLY BINDING OFFER FOR A VOLUNTARY TRANSFER

Even after the postal ballot result in May 2014, it took far longer than the Trust expected – another nineteen months in fact – to turn the draft offer into a legally binding offer (achieved in May 2015); and then to finalise the funding package and take ownership of the estate (achieved in December 2015). While no changes were made to the principles of the draft offer, it proved necessary over the course of the next year for lawyers to update some sections of the draft offer to take account of subsequent developments. A legally binding offer, incorporating provisions for these and other points, was signed by lawyers for the two sides on 7 May 2015.

The main points which had to be incorporated in the draft and final offers were:

- SSE's decision to withdraw from the sub lease with PRL in September 2014, having seemingly reached the conclusion that the wind farm was not going to receive approval. This required some factual updating of the terms of the offer. It was also agreed that, should another company take the place of SSE in the sub lease as seemed likely at the time, Barry Lomas would receive the same income from a commercial wind farm development as would have been the case under the SSE sub lease. The Pairc Trust insisted that this arrangement should only apply to a commercial wind farm, as defined in the offer, and only for the first twenty-five years. Any community owned wind turbines would not be subject to this condition. As it transpired, one of Nick Oppenheim's companies did not take the place of SSE in the wind farm sub lease as had at one time been envisaged, and the sub lease expired during 2015. This meant that, on taking ownership of the Pairc Estate land and leases, the Trust was under no obligation in relation to proceeding with any commercial wind farm.

- Dealing with the issue of VAT – the Trust (which had registered for VAT in 2014) had always assumed that no VAT would be payable on the purchase price of the estate. In the great majority of cases involving the sale of land no VAT is chargeable and in general land is not a commodity subject to VAT. However, it is the circumstances of the owner/vendor that dictates whether or not VAT is to be applied. But in early 2014 Barry Lomas indicated that, in his view, since he had exercised his option to tax in relation to the Pairc Estate, VAT would be payable unless HMRC granted a dispensation by treating the transaction as the transfer of a going concern. According to the Trust, he therefore insisted that provision for this should be made in the offer. This led to long, complex and costly discussions between professional accountants and lawyers acting on behalf of PCL, PRL and the Pairc Trust, with the involvement of HMRC (who ultimately had to decide whether VAT was payable or not in accordance with the legislation and guidelines under which it operated) and with CnES. The local authority agreed to provide a short term loan of £100,000 (20 per cent of the agreed purchase price of £500,000) to cover the eventuality that VAT would be payable, to deal with the cash flow problem the Trust might have faced over the period between paying the VAT on purchase and being able to reclaim it from HMRC.

The issue of the payment of VAT revolved round the question of whether the sale of the Pairc Estate would or would not be regarded by HMRC as a transfer of a going concern. HMRC, in accordance with its normal practice, would not give a ruling on this in advance of a claim. So it was necessary to include in the final offer several pages covering all eventualities, with additional money loaned from CnES which would be lodged in a separate bank account pending the outcome of HMRC's decision. The

situation involved additional risks for the Trust in that
it would have to make the claim to reclaim VAT and might
face a penalty charge by HMRC if the claim was judged
inadmissible. Moreover, there could be a delay in reclaiming
other VAT due to the Trust while the claim was being
considered. The VAT issue remained unresolved well after the
date of purchase of the estate, exacerbated by the fact
(according to the Trust) that there was a delay in Barry
Lomas providing evidence to HMRC that he had previously
exercised his option to tax in relation to the Pairc Estate.

- Confirming that the Crown Estate had no interest in the
foreshore of the Pairc Estate. There had been uncertainty
for many years as to whether the Pairc Estate did or did not
own the extensive foreshore around the coast of the estate.
This was a potentially valuable resource because of the
financial implications for rental from piers and wayleaves
etc. While Barry Lomas believed that the estate did include
the foreshore, there had been no confirmation that the
Crown Estate had relinquished its claim. The Trust therefore
entered into correspondence with the Crown Estate to clarify
the matter. In so doing, the Trust had to produce evidence
that the foreshore had historically been used by people living
in the area (for example for the harvesting of kelp – which
dated back to at least the eighteenth century). Eventually, the
Crown Estate Commissioners confirmed in May 2015 that it
had no interest in the Pairc Estate foreshore and it was
therefore made explicit in the offer that the foreshore was
part of the area to be purchased by the Pairc Trust.

- Incorporating a procedure for determining Barry Lomas's
reasonable level of professional fees incurred in finalising
the sale. Barry Lomas had made it clear from the earliest
discussions that he would not enter into a voluntary sale
of the estate if the costs he had incurred in the transaction
were not fully covered by the Pairc Trust. The Trust,
therefore, had agreed a commitment in the draft offer to
pay the legal and other professional fees 'reasonably,
necessarily, and properly incurred' by PCL and PRL in
negotiating, progressing and completing the transfer of
the Pairc Estate from 16 December 2013. This was one

of the conditions approved by the community in the
ballot of May 2014. However, with the passage of time, it
became evident to the Trust that a procedure would be
required to deal with any disagreement over the reasonable
level of fees. The right of remitting the issue for decision by
an appropriate neutral legal authority was therefore included.

A further factor contributing to the delay in the final stages was
the decision by Registers of Scotland that, before title to the Pairc
Estate could be registered in the name of the Pairc Trust, it was
necessary to produce a detailed map of the land to be purchased.
This included boundaries of over 270 pieces of land which had been
sold off within the Pairc Estate since the 1920s, many of which had
not been mapped at the time. Pairc Trust directors had to spend
substantial time over some six months in 2014 putting together
information from local people about individual areas of land
(typically around house sites) which had been sold off, sometimes
many years ago, and producing maps of the areas affected so that
internal boundaries within the Pairc Estate could be established
authoritatively. Maps setting out the proposed boundaries were
displayed by the Trust at the Ravenspoint Centre for public
comment in September 2014. In the case of previous community
buyouts of large estates, before Registers of Scotland changed
its policy, it had been possible to complete the detailed internal
mapping exercise after the title had been registered. While the
change in procedure contributed to the delay in taking ownership
of the estate, the Trust regarded Registers of Scotland as being
extremely helpful in all of the assistance it gave with the required
mapping.

THE LANDLORD'S CLAIMS FOR COMPENSATION UNDER PART 3 OF THE ACT

A further issue that took up considerable time was the landlord's
claims for compensation under Part 3 of the Land Reform (Scotland)
Act 2003. Under Section 89 of the Act, an owner or former owner
of land is entitled in particular circumstances to submit a claim for
compensation for loss or expense incurred. Barry Lomas (through
his companies PCL and PRL) exercised this right both in relation
to the Trust's 2005 Part 3 application (which was refused by the
Scottish Government in March 2011) and the two 2010 Part 3

applications (which were withdrawn by the Trust in December 2015 following the voluntary transfer of the estate in line with the terms of the agreed offer).

As regards the 2005 application, a compensation claim for over £750,000 was submitted to the Pairc Trust – or failing it the Scottish Government – in May 2010 under Section 89 (1) (a) and (b) of the Land Reform (Scotland) Act 2003. This section of the Act relates to circumstances where a crofting community body has made an application but withdrawn its confirmation to proceed or otherwise failed to complete the purchase. The claim was based on a fee note from Barry Lomas to PCL and PRL for services carried out in dealing with the Pairc Trust's application. The Trust pointed out that the claim was not competent because its 2005 application had not at that time been withdrawn or refused (it was still with Scottish Minsters for decision, even though the Trust regarded it as having been overtaken by its two new applications of February 2010). But, in any event, the Trust regarded the claim as excessive and invalid since, in its opinion, it was not necessary for Barry Lomas to have incurred most of the expenses, and because the claim was not properly vouched.

In rejecting the claim, the Trust used the word 'extort', which led to advice from Barry Lomas's lawyers that he would take legal action against directors of the Pairc Trust on the grounds that they had accused him of the criminal offence of extortion. The Trust issued an apology stating that there was no intention to accuse Mr Lomas of a criminal act. However, the Trust restated that in its view the claim was excessive and invalid.

Once Scottish Ministers had formally refused the Trust's 2005 Part 3 application in March 2011 (at the same time as approving the two new 2010 applications), the way was clear for Barry Lomas to submit claims for compensation to Ministers. This was done in mid June 2011, comprising three claims in relation to the 2005 application – one claim coming from PCL, one from PRL and one from Barry Lomas himself. It is understood that Scottish Government responded stating that none of the claims met the terms of the Act and the relevant regulations (The Crofting Community Right to Buy (Compensation) (Scotland) Order 2004). This, the author understands, was because the expenses claimed were insufficiently vouched and evidenced.

The Trust's two 2010 Part 3 applications remained in place throughout the later negotiations for a voluntary transfer of the estate. The terms of the agreed offer included provisions that the Pairc Trust: (a) would withdraw these Part 3 applications on completion of a voluntary purchase of the estate and (b) recognise the rights of PCL and PRL to submit a compensation claim against the Trust as provided for in Section 89 of the Act. These provisions were included on behalf of Barry Lomas. The Pairc Trust formally withdrew the Part 3 applications in December 2015. A further large compensation claim against the Trust was received in March 2016 from PCL and PRL under Sections 89 (1) (a) and (b) of the Act. The Trust made an initial response later in the same month, concluding that the claims failed to meet the relevant legal requirements in terms of section 89(1) of the Act and the accompanying regulations. This was followed up with a more detailed letter to Barry Lomas's solicitors dated 15 April 2016 which gave specific reasons for why the claim failed to meet the legal requirements – for example that the claims were not fully vouched, and that it was not clear that all the actions claimed for were required by the Act. No response was received within the 60 days specified in the regulations after which, failing agreement, either party could refer the matter to the Land Court. It is understood that no such reference to the Land Court has been made.

In conclusion, these compensation claims, while requiring much time and effort by Pairc Trust directors and their legal advisers, came to nothing. There can be little doubt that Barry Lomas would have spent a great deal of time in dealing with all aspects of the Trust's aspirations to acquire the Pairc Estate. However, the Part 3 compensation entitlement is confined only to costs which are in dealing with the Part 3 applications.

THE LANDLORD'S CLAIM FOR LEGAL AND PROFESSIONAL FEES

The last piece in the jigsaw puzzle before the voluntary transfer could be finalised was the determination of Barry Lomas's legal and other professional fees 'reasonably, necessarily, and properly incurred' from 16 December 2013 – which the Trust had agreed to pay as part of the final offer. While the Trust understood that other crofting communities had not paid the landlord's legal expenses when they purchased their estates on a voluntary basis, there were special circumstances in the case of Pairc. In particular, Barry Lomas would in principle have been able to claim compensation for reasonable expenses incurred in relation to a Part 3 purchase, and the Trust was in no doubt that he would not have agreed to a voluntary sale unless such a clause was included. The Trust ensured their commitment was only to 'reasonably, necessarily, and properly incurred' fees, and also that there was provision to appeal any disagreement over this to the Interim Auditor of the Court for the Sheriffdom of Grampian, Highlands and Islands. At the time the commitment was made, no-one on the Trust thought that it would take so long to complete the transaction, and an unfortunate consequence from the Trust's point of view was that it meant there was little or no pressure on the landlord to resolve issues speedily. Moreover, the Big Lottery Fund and Scottish Land Fund were unable to fund such expenses.

Once a legally binding offer had been agreed, the Trust received a claim from Barry Lomas on 13 May 2015 for his legal and other professional fees incurred in his part of the process of converting the Heads of Terms agreement into an acceptable legally binding offer. This included solicitors' fees incurred by PCL and PRL; and fee notes from Barry Lomas for professional services provided by himself and a firm of chartered accountants for specialist VAT advice to PCL and PRL. The Trust regarded the claim for legal and professional fees as excessive and unreasonable. It pointed out that its own legal and professional fees over the same period had been less than half that claimed by Barry Lomas. Also, the Trust believed that the time sheets he had submitted lacked detail on exactly what work was undertaken at the times specified. Taking into account all these factors, the Trust made an offer on 28 May 2015 in full and final settlement of the claim, but this was not accepted.

The Trust and Barry Lomas having failed to reach agreement on the level of fees consistent with the terms of the final offer, the matter was therefore the subject of a joint remit on 16 July 2015 to the Interim Auditor of the Court for the Sheriffdom of Grampian, Highlands and Islands, as provided for in the final offer. Both parties lodged written submissions and subsequently responded to his queries. Messrs Anderson MacArthur (solicitors to PCL and PRL) also forwarded their relevant files for inspection, along with

files from Barry Lomas. The Interim Auditor's decision was issued
on 5 November 2015. His determination was that Barry Lomas was
entitled to receive some £58,000 including VAT from the Pairc Trust
to cover his reasonable professional fees under the terms of the final
offer, a much lower figure than the claim submitted.

FINAL COSTS AND FUNDING PACKAGE

Once the level of professional fees due to Barry Lomas had been
determined, the Trust knew the total sum of money it would need to
secure in order to purchase the estate. It embarked on a final series
of discussions in November 2015 with the funding bodies, including
CnES and the Muaitheabhal Community Wind Farm Trust (MCWFT).
The Pairc Trust's own legal fees had also escalated because of the
time taken in bringing the voluntary purchase of the estate to a
conclusion since 2013. The Scottish Government therefore agreed
that the Scottish Land Fund (which was administered on its behalf
by the Big Lottery and HIE) could increase its grant for professional
fees from £50,000 to £70,000. This additional contribution from
central funding assisted the Trust in approaching CnES and MCWFT
for match funding to cover the remaining gap for legal fees. As
a result, CnES agreed to increase its grant to the Trust by an
additional £27,500 and MCWFT agreed to a loan of £27,500 (later
converted into a grant).

The final total package of grant and loan assistance towards the
capital cost of the purchase of the Pairc Estate (including allowance
for VAT) plus revenue funding for the first two years following
purchase was as follows:

Pairc Trust: £293,500

CnES: £212,000

Scottish Land Fund: £250,000

HIE: £76,500

MCWFT: £27,500

Total: £859,500

This funding was used as follows:

Estate purchase: £500,000

Legal and other professional fees: £120,000

VAT: £113,000

Revenue: £126,500

Total: £859,500

Finally – at long last – the Pairc Trust took ownership of the estate on behalf of the community on 4 December 2015.

CHAPTER 8: SUMMARY AND REFLECTIONS

The details of a voluntary transfer option, acceptable to both Barry Lomas and the majority of the board of Pairc Trust, were the subject of lengthy and complex negotiations between the two parties and required compromise on both sides. David Cameron's mediation role was crucial in facilitating discussion and the two sides reaching agreement on a voluntary transfer. Nick Oppenheim was also involved in aspects of the discussion. The advantages and disadvantages of pursuing the voluntary transfer option rather than trying to see through to completion the unfinished Part 3 route then needed careful explanation, consideration, and formal decision by both the Pairc Trust board and the wider Pairc community. This was concluded through a further non statutory postal ballot of the community counted on 1 May 2014, the result of which endorsed the recommendation of the Pairc Trust in favour of the voluntary transfer option.

But this was still not the end of the matter. It took a further eighteen months of detailed and complex work involving lawyers, accountants, and discussions with the funding bodies before the Pairc Trust and Barry Lomas agreed a legally binding offer for a voluntary transfer based on terms endorsed by the community and the Pairc Trust eventually taking ownership of the estate on behalf of the community. It was also necessary to deal with other issues such as the payment of VAT on the purchase price for the estate; claims by Barry Lomas for compensation in relation to the Trust's Part 3 applications; and for legal and other professional fees incurred in finalising the voluntary transfer. Detailed mapping of the estate in accordance with the standards set by, and with the considerable help of, Registers of Scotland was also required before title to Pairc Estate was finally transferred to the Pairc Trust in December 2015.

A few general points stand out:

- Although the eventual transfer of the estate was a voluntary one, it was never 'amicable' in the sense of there being goodwill between the seller and purchaser. This was the legacy of the earlier years of confrontation and mistrust. It probably also accounts significantly for why the final stages took much longer than expected by the Pairc Trust as disagreements continued right to the end over matters such as the landlord's Part 3 compensation claims and reasonably incurred legal fees.

- There were significant longer term knock-on consequences from these further delays for the Trust and the funding bodies. Support which had been agreed by funding bodies in 2014 or earlier in the expectation that the Trust would take ownership of the estate later that same year proved to be inadequate, given the increased revenue costs and escalating legal costs inevitably incurred by the Trust while the delays continued. The final funding package for the capital costs of purchasing the estate with revenue support for the Pairc Trust in the initial two years following purchase has been set out above. The Trust has made it known to the author that it is grateful for the flexibility shown by funding bodies in their responses to the delays incurred, although some of the problems caused by the delays, together with the continuing uncertainty over VAT, stored up problems for the Trust even after purchase of the estate.

- Finally, the difficult and complex choices which had to be made during 2013 and 2014, particularly over the terms of the voluntary transfer compared with continuing with the Part 3 approach, certainly exacerbated tensions within the Pairc Trust and to some extent the wider community. Some of these are touched on in the final chapter.

Nonetheless, despite all the frustrations and challenges, it should be emphasised that the Pairc Trust was ultimately successful in achieving community ownership of the estate. This was a notable achievement in the community land ownership movement. Hopefully it can be the trigger for substantial economic and social progress in Pairc in the years ahead.

The final chapter reflects on the long and tangled story of the Pairc buyout and attempts to draw out some overall conclusions and lessons for the future.

CHAPTER NINE

Overall Conclusions and Lessons Learned

Almost inevitably, this is a long chapter as there is a lot of ground to cover. In order to try to come to some sort of meaningful understanding of the long and complicated community buyout story it is considered useful to pose and attempt to answer a number of questions:

- What were the aims and motivations of the previous landlord, the Pairc Trust, and the local community?
- Why did the buyout take so long?
- Was the twin track strategy of the Pairc Trust the best one?
- What was the role of funding bodies and other organisations?

In addition, it is worth considering what lessons can be learned from the Pairc Trust buyout, particularly:

- For the Pairc Trust and the local community;
- For Government and land reform legislation; and
- For other communities involved in future buyouts

This account has been written very much from the crofting community's point of view, especially given that the previous landowner did not wish to contribute and therefore his views have not been able to be incorporated in it. The author does not want to hide the fact, however, that he supports the principle of community land ownership in circumstances where the majority in a community wish to proceed towards this outcome. In his view that does not mean this version of the history of the buyout is automatically biased in favour of one party and against the other. The author has no personal axe to grind against the previous landlord and has tried in his judgements to be as objective and even handed as possible. Whilst he has listened to and considered the views of many people, the conclusions are the author's, based on the evidence as he sees it.

WHAT WERE THE AIMS AND MOTIVATIONS OF THE PREVIOUS LANDLORD, PAIRC TRUST, AND THE LOCAL COMMUNITY?

Of course, there can be no hard and fast answers to this first question, only reasonable speculation as to key motivations. Ultimately it is for each reader to pick through this account of the buyout and to form a personal judgement. The author has also had to write this without the benefit of any input from the previous landowner.

Starting with the previous landlord (acting in a personal capacity or as a director of Pairc Crofters Ltd or Pairc Renewables Ltd) – it could appear that an over-riding motivation, or concern, throughout the whole period of the buyout was financial. It was not unreasonable for Barry Lomas to try to maximise the return he could achieve from the sale of the Pairc Estate assets. He was perfectly entitled to do this. But did he rely too much on his own judgement in determining what the value of those assets was rather than acting on independent valuation advice? If so, this could have led to over-optimistic and unrealistic expectations about the value of his assets and a position from which he may have been reluctant to move. Only when the inevitability regarding a Part 3 purchase was apparent did it appear that he was willing to compromise.

In the early years of the Pairc Trust he seemed to give out mixed messages about his willingness in principle to sell the estate. Certainly this is the interpretation that has been put to the author from a number of sources. But in practice he seemed to resist any form of community buyout, probably because he wished to retain ownership of the estate. This would ensure the estate generated a substantial monetary return for himself and his companies through a large, commercial wind farm in conjunction with SSE. His aim could be reasonably interpreted as being one of wanting to retain ownership of the land in the hope and expectation that the wind farm would receive consent from the Scottish Government, after which the value of his assets would greatly increase. Although other interpretations are possible, this motivation seems a plausible and reasonable explanation for why he established the subsidiary company of PRL and put in place an interposed lease between PCL and PRL; and then a sub lease between PRL and SSE for the development of the wind farm. These moves can also be reasonably interpreted as not only an attempt to safeguard his own interests but to impede, at the same time, the local community in its ambitions to purchase the estate. Acquisition of the land by the local community would have been virtually worthless and not worthwhile without also acquiring the landlord's interest in the interposed lease.

From at least 2013 onwards the landlord's aim could be reasonably interpreted as having broadened beyond focussing on the price which the Pairc Trust would have to pay to purchase the estate (and lease) to include recovering the significant legal and other costs which were claimed to have been incurred in dealing with the Pairc Trust's Part 3 applications and in finalising a voluntary transfer. Support for this line of thought may lie in the very large compensation claims which were submitted to the Pairc Trust and Scottish Government in relation to the costs claimed to have been incurred in dealing with the Trust's 2005 and 2010 Part 3 applications. As has been pointed out to the author, these were far in excess of the price received for the sale of the land and lease.

Roy Shearer – the solicitor acting for the Pairc Trust for most of the period – has told the author that he found it extraordinary that Barry Lomas could, on the face of it, have incurred losses in opposing the 2005 and 2010 Part 3 buyout applications amounting to well over the value he accepted for the whole estate. On the basis of Barry Lomas's own figures he would have made a big paper loss in transferring the Pairc Estate to the Trust by expending such large sums in trying to retain ownership of the land, even though the agreed purchase price of £500,000 was well above the estimate of some £300,000 made by the independent valuer. Under the legislation, Barry Lomas was always guaranteed to receive the full market value of the estate (and lease) as assessed either by an independent valuer or by the Scottish Land Court.

OVERALL CONCLUSIONS AND LESSONS TO BE LEARNED

Barry Lomas's attitude (and that of his family before him) towards crofting on the estate and local initiatives by the people of Pairc has been described to the author as being, at the best, generally passive and benign. The Pairc Trust, for example, has claimed on more than one occasion, that the landowner and the Lomas family has not created any jobs on the estate during the more than ninety years of the land having been in its ownership. The author is not aware of any challenge to this assertion. Even if the claim were not to be true, it is reasonable to share the sentiment, expressed to the author, that the estate did not flourish under the stewardship of the Lomas family. Like many other remote areas, the population total declined dramatically over that period. The area also suffered from deep social and economic problems, especially limited employment opportunities and poor community infrastructure. It would be unfair to lay all of this at the landlord's door. However, it does appear to be the case that the Lomas family were not in the vanguard of seeking or implementing remedies for a number of these problems during the long period that the estate and its people were under its stewardship.

It has also been put to the author that there may however have been a further motivation. Under this explanation, the Pairc community buyout process appears to have developed into something of a vendetta between Barry Lomas and the Pairc Trust – or, more strictly, between him and certain directors of the Trust. Neither side seemed prepared to give way. On occasions both parties produced written material highly critical of the other, and perhaps sometimes in language unhelpful to improving relationships between them. It may have been that at some point Barry Lomas's financial interests and considerations were augmented by a determination to defeat the Pairc Trust because of these personal factors. This latter point may have been equally true also from the point of view of some of the directors of the Pairc Trust. While this can only be speculation it seems to the author a plausible explanation. There could also have been an element of expectation on the part of Barry Lomas that the community and the Pairc Trust would become so frustrated by the sheer length and twists and turns of the buyout process that they would simply give up. In many ways it is surprising – perhaps even remarkable – that they did not do so. In no small measure that was probably due to some key individuals of whom Angus McDowall (a longstanding member of the Trust and its chairman at the time of writing) was perhaps the most prominent and influential person.

The main aim from the outset of the liaison group, the forerunner to the Pairc Trust, was to obtain the best possible terms for the local community from a commercial wind farm if one was developed. This soon broadened under the Pairc Trust to pursuing a community buyout of the estate. It should be recognised that the Pairc community is of course by no means a homogeneous body, and there was an obligation on the Trust to ensure at all times that it was acting in line with the wishes of the majority of residents. As regards community ownership, which was from early on always the main aim, there can be no doubt – as demonstrated in a succession of secret ballots – that this reflected the views of a large majority of Pairc residents. There was, and still is, a widely shared view that urgent and radical action is needed to address the social and economic problems of the area. The Trust's business plan – produced following community involvement and consultation – attempted to do just that. It set out ambitious proposals to create more local jobs, generate increased income for the area, provide more affordable housing, and improve community facilities for the benefit of all residents of Pairc.

A major if rarely articulated factor underlying support for the buyout was the conviction by a silent majority of native residents, whose families have lived in the wider Pairc area for many generations, that community ownership is not only a means of helping the economic and social regeneration of the district; but also of righting historic wrongs inflicted by previous landlords at the time of the Clearances (well before the Lomas family took ownership). The reasons for this fundamental bedrock support may not have been shared or appreciated by Barry Lomas or indeed some of the more recent incomers to Pairc. However, in the author's view, it helps to explain why the buyout story swiftly became what can be interpreted as a confrontation between irreconcilable aims.

While there can be no doubt from the results of the ballots that the aims of the Pairc Trust commanded the majority support of Pairc residents throughout, there were some alternative views. A significant minority were wary of community ownership in principle.

Some crofters were content with what had been regarded by them and some other local folk as a generally very passive approach by Barry Lomas and his family towards managing the estate. Those in this group were probably concerned that community control ran the risk of more pro-active management which was not necessarily in their own personal interests. It was also the case that a successful Part 3 buyout as proposed in the applications made by the Trust, would have had the unfortunate consequence of crofting tenants on the estate having two landlords (Barry Lomas for the in bye land and the Pairc Trust for the common grazings) for at least an initial and possibly a much longer period of indeterminate length. This certainly discouraged some crofters from voting in favour of a Part 3 buyout in the community ballots from what has been said to the author. Whilst crofters having two landlords would probably have made virtually little or no difference or inconvenience to their day to day management of their crofts (as they were only paying low rents for the in bye land and for their share in the common grazings), a number were known, (according to comments made to the author) to want a clean break from Barry Lomas as their landlord.

Others supported community ownership if it could be brought about by mutual agreement with the landlord, but objected to the compulsion involved under Part 3 of the Land Reform Act 2003. Some residents also seemed not to be confident that the Pairc Trust would be representative of the community as a whole (despite directors being democratically elected); or doubted that the community had the range of human resources to sustain the efficient management of the estate in the long term.

Indeed, some thought that the Trust was dominated by directors who favoured the commercial wind farm, and were even promoting it – because it was the case that some directors were crofters who stood to benefit personally financially from it. While the author saw no evidence that personal gain was a motivating factor for any of the directors, there is no doubt that the commercial wind farm proposal was a highly divisive factor which led to difficulties and misunderstandings within the Pairc community in the early years of Pairc Trust. Some people, including many in the more recent incoming community, did not support the Trust because they opposed the wind farm and believed that the Trust was promoting it. Over time, as the immediate prospect of a large commercial wind farm receded, opposition to the Pairc Trust and its aims on these grounds appeared generally to reduce.

WHY DID THE BUYOUT TAKE SO LONG?

The main reason, from views the author has gathered, was that for many years Barry Lomas simply did not appear to wish to sell the Estate at a price the Trust believed was reasonable – at least up to around 2013. While this view may not be universally shared and might be challenged by some, including Barry Lomas, it is the author's conclusion based on consideration of the material that was available for his research. If Barry Lomas was open in principle at the outset to a voluntary transfer of the estate it is possible that the Pairc Trust's decision to hold a ballot in 2004 and submit a Part 3 application changed his mind from that point onwards. The prospect of a Part 3 application was possibly also a critical factor in his decision to establish the interposed lease. In the author's view it was probably only after the Court of Session's comprehensive rejection in December 2012 of the first part of his appeal against the Government's approval of the Trust's Part 3 applications, that he seemed to accept that a buyout was inevitable; and thereafter focussed on achieving the most favourable financial settlement possible.

With hindsight, the relationship between the two parties seems to have been soured irrevocably from around mid 2004. Personality clashes between Barry Lomas and some Pairc Trust directors appear to have been a significant factor. This could well have been important in the decision and timing to establish the interposed lease in August 2004 (though the Trust was not notified of its existence until February 2005) though without input from Barry Lomas this can only be speculation.

A number of actions by or on behalf of Barry Lomas resulted in considerable delays to the outcome of the community buyout of the estate. For example, the interposed lease (which the Government referred to the Land Court in 2005); the unsuccessful petition to the Court of Session in April 2010 for interim suspension of the Government's acceptance of the 2010 Part 3 applications as being valid for consultation; the submissions relating to the Part 3 applications during the statutory consultation period later in 2010;

and the appeal against the Government's decision taken in March 2011 to approve the applications.

During some of the periods when Barry Lomas entered into discussions with the Trust about a voluntary transfer of the Estate (for example between summer 2007 and summer 2009), he may have been content that agreement was not reached all the time there was a chance that the commercial wind farm proposal would be approved. But again, without his input this can only be speculation. It was put to the author that the Trust came to the conclusion in retrospect that Barry Lomas had been 'stringing it along' rather than engaging in serious discussions about selling the estate. Also, throughout the buyout discussions, the author has been told by a number of people (by no means all connected to the Pairc Trust) that Barry Lomas appeared to find it difficult to take and commit to decisions. If so, this may also have been a further factor in the delays.

The prospect of a substantial wind farm being developed on part of the estate fluctuated, and alternately waxed and waned over a long time period. It was far from being a linear progression. Until the outcome of the commercial wind farm proposal had been reached (and the Court of Session ruling) there was a powerful financial incentive for Barry Lomas not to agree to a voluntary transfer of the estate.

Without the wind farm proposal he may well have been a more willing seller; and the transfer of ownership of the estate could have taken place more quickly. It also has to be said that without the prospect of a wind farm the Pairc community in 2003 is unlikely to have been interested in a buyout of the estate at that point in time. However, the author has been told by a number of people that given the activity and success of other community land trusts such as in South Uist, North Harris and Galson it would only have been a matter of time before the Pairc community would have wished to own the estate.

Another possible factor influencing the length of time for the buyout could have been a lack of relevant and necessary negotiating experience and skills on both sides. The Pairc case was highly complex and technical. Although both sides had access to professional advice, nevertheless the two parties were responsible for undertaking most of the discussions and negotiations. Inexperience on both sides may therefore have been a contributory factor in prolonging the buyout.

It is also relevant that no time limits applied to several of the legal processes which proved necessary to deal with these matters, and, therefore, in practice lengthy delays ensued. For example, the Scottish Land Court took approaching two years (autumn 2005 – summer 2007) to issue a decision on the status of the interposed lease. It took a little over one year from the submission of the 2010 Part 3 applications (February 2010) for Scottish Ministers to issue a decision (March 2011). It was not until December 2012, some eighteen months after Barry Lomas's decision to appeal against the Government's approval of these applications that the Court of Session came to a judgement on the first part of his appeal. It took nearly six months for the Interim Auditor to determine a reasonable level of professional fees following the claim submitted to the Trust by Barry Lomas in May 2015.

It also took a lengthy period of time (some eighteen months) to complete the legal documentation for the purchase of the estate following the Pairc community's endorsement through a postal ballot on 1 May 2014 of the draft agreement reached between Barry Lomas and the Pairc Trust. This was because several issues (for example, the possibility raised by Barry Lomas of VAT payments on the sale of the estate) became the subject of long and detailed legal negotiation before resolution to the satisfaction of both parties. A legally binding agreement was only eventually signed by solicitors on behalf of the two parties on 7 May 2015, a full year after the community's endorsement of the terms, and it was a further seven months before the Trust finally took ownership of the estate in December 2015.

A further factor contributing to the delay in the final stages was the decision by Registers of Scotland (RoS) that, before title to the Pairc Estate could be registered in the name of the Pairc Trust, it was necessary to produce a detailed map of the land to be purchased. This included the boundaries of over 270 pieces of land which had been sold off within the estate from 1924 onwards, many of which had not been mapped at the time. In previous community buyouts, RoS had allowed the detailed mapping to take place after transfer of title. While the Trust was very grateful for the help given it by RoS in completing the mapping exercise, this change of policy contributed to the delay.

WAS THE TWIN TRACK STRATEGY OF THE PAIRC TRUST THE BEST ONE?

The author has been told that the Trust's twin track approach was never an either/or choice but a considered strategy to use Part 3 as a lever to achieve a buyout either through a voluntary transfer or, failing that, through a Part 3 application (which did not involve Barry Lomas being a willing seller). Through the Part 3 route he could be forced to sell at market value provided the Trust could meet the legislative criteria (which, by March 2011, it was known it could), subject to the outcome of Barry Lomas's appeal. It was always the Trust's preferred option, however, to achieve a voluntary transfer of the whole estate (and the interposed lease when that came to light) at what it considered to be a reasonable price and on reasonable terms. However, it seemed to the Trust from early on that Barry Lomas was unwilling to sell the estate (and subsequently the lease) on a voluntary basis on terms and at a price which were acceptable to it. The complicating factor was, of course, the prospect of a commercial wind farm from which he would have obtained a significant financial return via PCL and PRL.

It may well be that (as already indicated) Barry Lomas might have been willing in principle early on to consider a voluntary transfer of the estate. However, if that was so, the Pairc Trust's decision to submit a Part 3 application may have changed Barry Lomas's mind. Be that as it may, the prospect of major financial gain from a commercial wind farm seems likely to have been in Barry Lomas's mind from the outset. It seems unlikely therefore, with the benefit of hindsight, that Barry Lomas would have agreed a voluntary transfer without insisting on a high purchase price – probably far more than the Trust would have considered to be reasonable and probably considerably in excess of any independent valuation.

In 2004 the Pairc Trust and the local community decided to embark on a Part 3 application confined to the crofting common grazings only (thereby omitting the crofting in bye land and also the Steimreway grazings which were outwith crofting tenure and leased under an agricultural tenancy). This was done essentially for pragmatic reasons, given the difficulty of mapping the in bye land in accordance with the onerous requirements of the legislation. The thinking was that if the Part 3 application for the common grazings was successful then Barry Lomas might be prepared to enter into a voluntary sale for the remaining areas. If not then the Trust could submit a further Part 3 application at a later stage provided it could overcome the perceived difficulties of mapping the land in the detail required by the 2003 Act.

Most (though not all) Pairc Trust directors saw progress under Part 3 as the best way of bringing pressure to bear on the landlord to enter into realistic negotiations for a voluntary transfer. Ultimately, this proved to be correct despite the time it took and the amount paid for the estate and lease by the Trust. While Barry Lomas claimed that the twin track approach was duplicitous, the threat of returning to the Part 3 route was undoubtedly (in the author's view) the key in enabling the Trust to negotiate what most of its directors and also the majority of the local community (as shown in the ballot result announced on 1 May 2014) considered an acceptable voluntary outcome. Indeed, the only real negotiating lever the Trust had was resort to the Part 3 approach or the threat to return to it if talks had broken down in the latter stages of the process in 2014 and 2015.

The author's view (based on the information he has gathered) is that the price and terms of the eventual voluntary purchase were almost certainly the most favourable that the Pairc Trust could have obtained. Barry Lomas, it seems, is unlikely to have accepted less and the Trust would not have been able to negotiate the terms achieved had it not been for the threat of Part 3. It is also the case that, since the eventual purchase price was significantly greater than that of independent valuations (which determined how much support it could receive from the public sector), the Trust was only able to fund the purchase because of the substantial sum it received from Eishken Nominees Ltd (one of Nick Oppenheim's companies involved in the Eishken wind farm developments) as a result of the agreement on a right of access over the Eishken road.

It is, of course, quite legitimate to query whether the Trust was correct in the emphasis it gave to the two approaches at particular times over the whole thirteen year period. For example, it can be argued that the Trust should have called a halt to the voluntary discussions between 2007 and 2009 much earlier than it did. Nonetheless, overall, it seems to the author that the twin track approach was the optimum strategy to have adopted. Neither approach was completely abandoned until the very end of the story in December 2015 when a purchase based on a voluntary transfer was legally finalised and the outstanding Part 3 applications subsequently withdrawn (as agreed in the terms of the legal agreement).

WHAT WAS THE ROLE OF FUNDING BODIES AND OTHER ORGANISATIONS?

The Pairc Trust had contact with a number of funding bodies and other organisations (apart from the Scottish Government) during the long course of the buyout. These included: Highlands and Islands Enterprise (HIE); Big Lottery Fund and the Scottish Land Fund; Comhairle nan Eilean Siar (CnES); Muaitheabhal Community Wind Farm Trust (MCWFT); and Community Land Scotland (CLS).

All were supportive of the Pairc Trust's aims, and played an important part in enabling its main aim to be achieved, while of course needing to have regard to the legislation and internal rules by which their own activities are governed. The contribution made by funding bodies to the final package of capital and revenue support has been set out in chapter eight.

HIE gave the Trust considerable helpful advice, moral support, and substantial funding towards its own legal costs over many years. This comprised continuing support for ongoing legal costs over an unexpectedly long period which was, no doubt, unusual and a challenge for HIE given the financial guidelines it worked under. This revenue support, over an unusually long period, was essential to the eventual outcome. HIE also provided further revenue funding for the first two years after purchase and, with the Big Lottery Fund, also administered the Scottish Land Fund which provided financial support for the purchase of the estate and towards professional fees. The main contact in HIE at official level throughout the whole period of the buyout was Sandra Holmes. The author is aware that the Trust is extremely grateful to her (and all her colleagues) for the advice and support given.

The Scottish Land Fund was re-established by the Scottish Government during the course of the buyout, with its administration carried out by HIE and the Big Lottery Fund. The author is aware that the Pairc Trust is grateful to David Knight and other officials concerned for their helpful and flexible approach, within the guidelines under which they operated, in coping with the consequences of the delay which occurred between the initial award of SLF funding in 2013 and the date when the Trust eventually took ownership of the estate.

Throughout the thirteen years of the buyout, the Pairc Trust believes that no outside body was more helpful in the generous and unstinting support it gave at all levels (officers and members) over the whole period than the local authority for the Western Isles, Comhairle nan Eilean Siar (CnES). Community ownership is central to the Comhairle's economic strategy for the islands, and from the Convener down, the Trust believes that CnES could not have been more supportive. The Trust has drawn the author's attention to the particular contribution of the Comhairle's main officer-level contact – Calum Iain MacIver, Director of Development – but other officials such as Joe MacPhee, Robert Emmott and Chief Executive Malcolm Burr were also extremely helpful and supportive at all stages.

MCWFT was established in 2012 with money from the Eishken wind farm development. From this point onwards, the Trust regarded MCWFT as an obvious potential source of funding to help with the buyout – Pairc forming a significant part of the area that MCWFT was set up to assist. Although the Trust's application for funding in November 2015 (to help top up the funding package once the level was known of Barry Lomas's professional fees as determined by the Interim Auditor) was not straightforward, the Trust was awarded a loan (later converted into a grant) of £27,500. This was of considerable assistance to the Trust in finalising the financial package to purchase the estate in December 2015. The Trust has made the author aware of its gratitude to MCWFT for this help and in particular to its chairman, Iain MacIver of Laxay.

The Pairc Trust became a member of CLS from the start when the organisation was established in 2009. Under the chairmanship of David Cameron from Harris (subsequently Lorne Macleod from Oban), CLS quickly became influential in political circles and a useful source of moral support for community ownership, including the Trust's own buyout. In addition, as described in chapter seven, David Cameron, acting in a personal capacity, played an invaluable role in mediating between the Trust and Barry Lomas which eventually led to the voluntary transfer of the estate into community ownership.

WHAT LESSONS CAN BE LEARNED FROM THE BUYOUT BY THE PAIRC TRUST AND THE LOCAL COMMUNITY?

Although the Trust certainly tried to keep the local community up to date with developments over the long period of the buyout (principally through public meetings, newsletters, and the Trust's website) it is clear that it was not always successful in achieving this. Some in the local area came to regard the Pairc Trust as rather remote and uninformative. Others had misunderstandings about the aims and policy position of the Trust and were ready to attribute unflattering motives to some of its directors.

In defence of the Trust, it should be recognised that the legal and financial complexity of the situation (for example the different considerations applying to the Part 3 applications and the voluntary transfer discussions) made it very difficult to provide summary statements which were genuinely informative and did not breach confidentialities. Moreover, the very length of time of the buyout process made it difficult to sustain the enthusiasm and interest of the community at anything like the level of the early years of the Trust. It was a common perception that nothing much was happening, even though directors were immersed almost throughout the thirteen years of the buyout in often highly complex and sensitive discussions.

The challenges faced by the Trust in working with the local community, keeping people up to date with developments and avoiding misunderstandings, are common to many community organisations, including other community landowners. Even organisations which have clearly brought about great improvements in the economic fortunes of their local communities (for example Stòras Uibhist, North Harris Trust and the Galson Estate Trust) have faced criticisms on this score. There are almost always some individuals or groups within a local community who are suspicious of or hostile towards other members or organisations within the community, whether as a result of personal disagreements in the past or justified complaints about the way decisions are taken and how these affect others in the community. Indeed, the tendency for local disputes often to be more acrimonious when the decision makers are local people known to almost everyone in the community (rather than say more 'anonymous' government organisations or landlords not resident in the area) is a well known phenomenon which is an important aspect of the debate about the advantages and disadvantages of community land ownership.

What made the task of the Pairc Trust even more difficult was the apparent lack of progress with the buyout over so many years, the many legal disputes which arose, and the confidential nature of much of the ongoing negotiation process with Barry Lomas. Even though most of the delay was due to factors outside the control of the Trust there was an understandable tendency for some in the community to attribute part of the responsibility for it to the Pairc Trust. This can be said perhaps particularly of people who were suspicious or mistrustful of some of the directors. Against this background, it is perhaps remarkable that the Trust retained the confidence and backing of the majority in the community over such a long drawn out period, as seen in the results of successive ballots.

That is not to say that the Pairc Trust could or should not have done more to improve communications. There were times when the gaps between public meetings or newsletters and other information bulletins were too long. On other occasions perhaps more information could have been made available to the local community without breaking confidentiality issues. In the author's experience it is almost always possible to improve communications, and learn lessons from experience.

Now that the Pairc Trust has taken ownership of the estate, it is clearly essential that it redoubles its efforts to involve others in the community, consult closely with local people and take them with it on key decisions. In going forward, more effort needs to be given by the Trust to communicate better and more frequently with the local community. It should also try to improve two way information flows with local people and other local organisations so that decisions by the Pairc Trust board are better informed by local opinion.

Turning to the Trust's internal procedures and practices, some of these could almost certainly have been improved. Again, some of the difficulties go to the heart of the challenges facing community ownership – do small crofting communities have the human resources and range of experience necessary to negotiate the purchase of large estates and then manage them in an efficient way? In the case of Pairc, the complexity of the issues facing the Trust directors (all unpaid volunteers) was huge, requiring a knowledge of (amongst other things) land reform legislation which had never been used before, crofting law, the workings of central and local Government and funding agencies, the legal procedures and financial issues affecting commercial scale wind farms, governance issues relating to charities and community organisations, negotiating skills, and the conduct of meetings.

This was a tall order for a community of some 400 people in rural Lewis and there is no doubt that the Trust was severely challenged on occasions. For most of the life of the Trust there have been vacancies for directors which have proved difficult to fill. Consequently elections for directors have been rarely contested, and representation from the community not as complete as would have been useful. In particular it has been difficult to attract young people and women on to the board. Overall, however, despite the shortcomings, it is remarkable, in the author's view, that the Trust has done as well as it has and eventually delivered a successful outcome. Furthermore, it should be borne in mind that negotiations were always more complex for the Trust than for Barry Lomas, since the Trust had to form a collective view (and regularly consult the community either formally or informally). This inevitably took more time and was more difficult than a single person being effectively in control of and negotiating on behalf of an organisation which was the case with Barry Lomas.

The burden of running the Trust fell mainly on the shoulders of a few volunteer directors, particularly the office bearers. The key directors had some expertise in Government administration and public funding agencies, private construction companies, crofting, and renewable energy. There was a good knowledge of the local community and the Trust was able to buy in professional legal and accounting advice. While these resources enabled the Trust to function reasonably effectively and indeed bring about an ultimately successful outcome, it frequently had to rely on the experience of just one or two directors on particular topics. Therefore genuine discussion at board level seems often to have been limited and it also seems certain that the conduct of many meetings could have been improved. There were occasions when the gap between board meetings was longer than it should have been, with the result that some directors felt out of touch with the latest developments in the negotiations.

Despite this, the Memorandum and Articles of Association (prepared with professional advice and which have been updated from time to time) were consistent with guidelines approved by the Scottish Government for community bodies. By 2008, the board had also introduced a Code of Conduct for directors which all directors were required to sign on appointment. An independent review by Third Sector Hebrides in January 2015 concluded that the governance arrangements for the Trust were satisfactory, and that the Code of Conduct in particular was an example of best practice. Advice was also given on the duties of directors and the chairing of meetings. In line with recommended best practice, the Trust established a subsidiary company Pairc Trading Ltd in May 2015 as a vehicle for taking forward projects after purchasing the estate.

Through his research the author has come across a particularly difficult episode involving the Pairc Trust board which revolved around an internal dispute between one director and the others. This came to a head in the summer of 2015. The origins of the dispute appear to go back to 2013 when the board took the decision to recommend to the community that priority should be given to pursuing the option of a voluntary transfer of the estate into community ownership rather than following a Part 3 route.

Following that decision in November 2013 and its endorsement in a ballot in May 2014 by the local community, the author has been told that the director in question attempted to re-open discussion on it on a number of occasions on the grounds that there had been material changes in the situation. The rest of the Pairc Trust board did not accept that any changes which had occurred (for example, SSE's decision to withdraw from the sub lease in September 2014) justified reconsidering the decision.

It was of course perfectly reasonable for a director to have taken a different view from that of the other Pairc Trust directors prior to the board's formal decision and its subsequent endorsement by the community. However, after that point the board held that all directors should have respected and supported the majority decision (endorsed by the community) in line with the principles of collective responsibility enshrined in the Pairc Trust Directors' Code of Conduct.

It is clear to the author that the Trust should have taken more decisive action at a much earlier stage to resolve the matter and to ensure that the director either accepted the decision or stepped down from the board.

The author understands that the episode has left a legacy of mistrust and bad feelings which to an extent still seems to cause or exacerbate some problems within parts of the Pairc local community today.

It is not unusual that local community organisations are faced with internal differences of view among their directors or members. In small rural communities in particular, these sometimes can be among some of the most difficult challenges that organisations have to face. The Pairc Trust episode appears to have been more painful and longer lasting than most.

There is a lesson that can be learnt from this by other communities and not just Pairc. It is that the full benefits of community – led initiatives (such as community land ownership) can best be realised if the community works and pulls together. This requires sensitive but clear leadership from community leaders with a lot of effort to ensure full and genuine consultation with everyone, effective communication, and a will to listen and change views in the light of local feedback. It also needs the whole community to work together once key decisions have been properly and democratically taken. In Pairc the author believes that somehow the Trust and the local community now needs to find a way to put this episode behind it and move on for the greater good.

WHAT LESSONS CAN BE DRAWN FOR GOVERNMENT AND LAND REFORM LEGISLATION?

There are many lessons to be drawn from the Pairc buyout case for Government and for land reform legislation. The Court of Session ruling in December 2012 has already had an impact on the climate of opinion concerning the circumstances in which Government is legally justified in granting communities the right to apply to buy privately owned land. There has also been wide recognition that the procedures which Pairc Trust was required to follow in making its applications under Part 3 of the Land Reform (Scotland) Act 2003 were unreasonably complicated and need to be simplified. These views are already reflected in a number of pieces of new legislation introduced by the Scottish Government in more recent years, although in the author's opinion some further changes are still required.

Looking first at the justification for Government intervention in the private land market on behalf of community interests, David Cameron of Community Land Scotland is of the opinion that the Pairc Estate buyout has had a huge effect. He believes that the Court of Session ruling in December 2012 was a key development in the realisation by estate owners across Scotland that their property rights were not absolute. So, whilst they could challenge government in court they were not guaranteed to win. The court case resulted in Scottish Government officials being able to have more confidence that the provisions in Part 3 of the Land Reform (Scotland) Act 2003 were legally robust, and this paved the way through the Community Empowerment (Scotland) Act 2015 for provisions to be introduced giving all communities in Scotland in certain circumstances the right to apply to buy land when there was not a willing seller where they could show that land was 'abandoned, neglected or detrimental' as defined in the legislation and subsequent regulations. A further change was made by the Land Reform (Scotland) Act 2016 enabling provisions to be introduced to give communities throughout Scotland the right to apply to buy land to further sustainable development.

A further consequence of the Pairc case is that it has made it easier for other communities to negotiate land sales in the shadow of the law as landowners now realise that their property rights are not absolute and that they might lose any challenge to Ministerial decisions to grant the right to buy to a community. The Court of Session in the Pairc case ruling also led to a protocol on the voluntary sale of land between Community Land Scotland and Scottish Land and Estates (SLE). And the experience in Pairc, beyond the court case, also led to the law now incorporating a power to Ministers in relation to the arrangement or facilitation of mediation services.

Turning now to the detailed procedures which the Pairc Trust was required to follow under Part 3 of the Land Reform (Scotland) Act

2003, the Trust believes and would wish to acknowledge that both Ministers and civil servants in the Scottish Government were as supportive as possible throughout the buyout within the limits of their necessary neutrality and responsibilities under the existing legislation. However, the Trust also believes that Part 3 of the Land Reform (Scotland) Act 2003 had significant flaws, not all of which have yet been rectified. The main points have already been made to Scottish Government either directly by the Trust or by Community Land Scotland.

In summary, the procedures which the Pairc Trust had to follow to exercise its rights to purchase crofting land and the related leases:

- Were extremely complex and time-consuming;
- Sometimes seemed to have no relevant purpose; and
- Risked legal challenge on minor technical grounds

The issues can best be understood by consideration of the application form for consent to buy eligible croft land (or the interest of the tenant in related tenanted land), which was prescribed by secondary legislation. It is, of course, perfectly reasonable that a crofting community body should be required to:

- Demonstrate that it is properly constituted and represents the relevant crofting community;
- Define the boundaries of the land or lease it seeks to buy;
- Prove that the majority in the community (both crofters and non crofters) support the application; and
- Provide evidence that it is in the public interest that it should be given permission to buy the land or interest of the tenant.

However, there seems no logical or functional rationale for having been required to provide the following:

- A map and written description showing not only the boundary of the land or lease to be acquired, but also all sewers, pipes, lines, watercourses or other conduits, and fences, dykes, ditches, or other boundaries. This went far beyond what is required in other land or lease transactions, and there seems no functional reason to have required this information. It was particularly onerous and seemingly absurd when the area to be purchased extended to well over 20,000 acres;
- A list of all postcodes and Ordnance Survey one kilometre

grid squares included in the land or lease area to be
purchased. Again there seems no reason for this if the
boundary was properly defined on a map. If the area
concerned extends to many thousands of acres, the list
simply opens up scope for a technical challenge if particular
postcodes or grid squares are inadvertently omitted;

- The extensive details required about each member of the
crofting community eligible to vote in the ballot. These
details have since been amended by the Community
Empowerment (Scotland) Act 2015. In the author's view,
the key test should be that a majority in the community
supports the application, rather than having to provide
detailed lists which opens up the possibility of a legal
challenge if any error or inconsistency is made.

The Trust's view was that a criterion of proportionality should have
been explicitly applied to all such provisions (if indeed they were
to be retained at all) so that an application which met the essential
purposes of the Act was not at risk of refusal or legal challenge
on minor technical details. For example, an error in a very small
number of voters wrongly issued with ballot papers should not
invalidate the result if there is a large majority in favour. And an
error in the listing of a very small number of postcodes or grid
squares should not invalidate an application if the boundary of the
land or lease to be acquired is clear.

In fact, some minor factual errors were made in the Pairc
Trust's 2010 Part 3 applications. These came to light during the
consultation period and were taken into account when Ministers
approved the applications. Not all relevant postcodes and one
kilometre grid squares were listed correctly. And a very small
number (five) of Pairc residents received ballot papers because they
were on the current electoral roll but were under eighteen at the
time of the ballot. Clearly, this would not have affected the overall
result of the ballot in favour of the Pairc Trust's proposals, given
the large majority in favour. Such minor errors were amongst the
reasons listed in the second part of Barry Lomas's appeal against the
Scottish Government's decision in 2011 to approve the applications.
This part of his appeal never reached the Sheriff Court for a
judgement so it remains to be seen whether the Sheriff would have

upheld the appeal on what would be technical grounds. But there would certainly have been some risk that this perverse result might have happened.

Following these representations to the Scottish Government from the Trust and others, the Community Empowerment (Scotland) Act 2015 repealed Section 73(5)(b)(ii) of Part 3 of the Land Reform (Scotland) Act, so removing the requirement for community bodies to provide detailed information on sewers, pipes, lines, etc. However, the provisions requiring lists of postcodes, Ordnance Survey 1 km grid squares, and a list of all those eligible to vote in a ballot appear in the crofting community right to buy application form, which is prescribed in secondary legislation. Any amendments to these requirements (which in the author's view should be removed or simplified) would therefore require new legislation. In 2017 Ministers asked the Scottish Land Commission to review the effectiveness of the community right to buy mechanisms and it may be that they will await the Commission's findings before taking decisions.

When reviewing further legislative amendments to the Land Reform (Scotland) Act, consideration should also be given by the Scottish Government to whether the maximum length of time (i) between holding a community ballot and submitting a Part 3 application; and (ii) between Government approval of an application and purchase of the estate by the community are adequate now that Registers of Scotland require detailed mapping of the land before a purchase can be registered and title can change hands. Moreover, if (as now seems to be the case) a detailed map of the area to be purchased (including identification of small decrofted areas within the in bye land) has to be produced at the time an application is made to Government, this could (depending on circumstances) involve significant expense for the community body at a time when there is no guarantee that the application will be approved.

There are also further improvements that Community Land Scotland would like to see to the legislative and policy framework. In particular CLS would like to see powers given to Ministers to test where the public interest lies in any new land purchases – an effective veto on purchases if the new owner could not pass a public interest test as to the proposed uses of the land.

In the author's view, the sorts of public interest tests sought by Community Land Scotland to be applied to private land situations and private landowners would provide a useful counterbalance to the requirements that have to be met by crofting communities under Part 3 of the 2003 Act. At the same time, greater Scottish Government and local government policy encouragement for the repopulation of land would be of considerable benefit to a large number of crofting communities in the Highlands and Islands.

WHAT CAN OTHER COMMUNITIES INVOLVED IN FUTURE BUYOUTS LEARN FROM THE PAIRC ESTATE CASE?

It should be recognised that the Pairc Trust case was extreme in that a number of exceptional factors applied. The landlord seemed for much of the time to oppose the community's wish to buy the estate. He put in place an interposed lease, and appeared to do everything he could to prevent a successful Part 3 application. The Pairc commercial wind farm proposal divided opinion in the community and probably led to the landlord having an unrealistic view of the price he expected to receive for sale of the estate, even when the prospects for the wind farm receded. There was a damaging breakdown in trust between the two sides. And by pioneering the Part 3 process, which was followed further by Pairc Trust than by any other community body, the Pairc case exposed some serious flaws in the legislation.

Nonetheless, other communities considering purchase of their estates need to be aware of the factors which complicated matters for Pairc Trust, even if hopefully no other community will have to face all these obstacles. Indeed, other communities should now be able to benefit from the Pairc experience. The Part 3 legislation has now been tested (up to a point) and the Court of Session judgement has confirmed that the legislation is consistent with the European Convention on Human Rights. Also, as a result of the Pairc case, a number of changes have been made to Part 3 of the Land Reform Act designed to simplify matters for future community buyouts.

Despite these improvements, it needs to be recognised that the Part 3 route could still be long, complicated, time consuming, costly and full of uncertainties, with a timetable outwith the control of the local community or crofting community body. It is very demanding in terms of the range of skills required within a local community to achieve a successful outcome, even with considerable input from other organisations in relation to funding, legal advice, etc. It is probably best used as part of a twin track approach alongside negotiations for a voluntary transfer, as was the case with the Pairc Trust.

Even if it is regarded as an option of last resort, Part 3 remains the only means by which a crofting community can buy the land it occupies if the landowner is unwilling to sell for whatever reasons. While negotiation of a voluntary transfer is probably almost always preferable, this may not always appear to be an option. The Part 3 approach offers a lever, which is now more credible in the light of the Pairc case, to encourage a landlord to engage in serious discussions with a view to a voluntary transfer. Even if a Part 3 approach is used, it would be unwise in most circumstances for a local community to abandon negotiations for a voluntary transfer completely. In theory, a voluntary transfer and a Part 3 application should produce the same result for both parties, namely a sale at market value. In most cases, a market value will be relatively easily ascertainable so that there would be no reason for a landowner not to agree a voluntary transfer at this price, as has happened (so far as the author is aware) in all the other crofting community buyout cases apart from Pairc.

While the Pairc case demonstrates the need for leadership and persistence, it also highlights the crucial importance of consulting the community at all stages and avoiding damaging splits in the community if at all possible. The full benefits of community ownership will only be realised if the community is united, and the community body leading the buyout enjoys the trust of all sections of the community and is able to attract a good cross-section of volunteers from the community to act as Directors.

FINAL OBSERVATIONS

There are a few final observations and thoughts that should be set down on the whole Pairc saga. It was indeed a long and tangled story, which took up far more time and energy than should have been necessary. Only time will tell if it was all worthwhile – through community ownership bringing real benefits to the people of Pairc, including generations to come. The author hopes and believes this will be the case.

It is doubtful, in the author's opinion, in view of all of the
circumstances that the Pairc Trust could have done anything
much different in terms of its strategy which would have speeded
up things significantly. Faced with a landlord who it seems was
fundamentally not willing to sell at a price which reflected
independent valuations – who was prepared to put a lot of effort
(and money) into opposing the wishes of the large majority of the
community – and with legislation which was onerous and flawed, it
is perhaps remarkable that the Trust and the Pairc local community
succeeded in purchasing the estate. That the Trust eventually
achieved its main aim was due principally to the stamina and
determination of the various directors over a number of years and
also because of the tenacity of the local community.

Before the buyout began Barry Lomas was not generally regarded
as a bad landlord by the local community in the sense that, for
example, Eigg residents perceived their landlord. However, the
atmosphere between the two parties quickly became difficult and
often hostile over a number of issues stemming from the proposed
commercial wind farm. Both sides took up positions from which
they probably found it difficult to shift. This was not conducive to
reaching an amicable or quick settlement acceptable to both parties.
And both became mistrustful of the other.

It is difficult to see how the process could have been significantly
truncated until the outcome of the wind farm proposal had been
resolved. And that took an inordinate length of time. A voluntary
transfer at a price acceptable to Barry Lomas (which was well
above the level of independent valuations and therefore not wholly
fundable by public sector bodies) was only possible due to the good
fortune of the Pairc Trust receiving a large sum of money from
the Eishken road access agreement. Without that money the Trust
would have had to embark on a further round of private fundraising
with no certainty of meeting its target. David Cameron was also
instrumental in unlocking the deadlock between the two sides.

The real tragedy of the length of time it took to purchase the
estate is the legacy it left: a community whose enthusiasm for the
opportunities of ownership has been sapped by the long grind
of dealing with problems and opposition to the purchase. Other
communities have bought their estates much more quickly while
the initial enthusiasm was still strong and this has carried through

to the demanding challenges of running the estate and making a difference to people's lives. The Pairc community is really just at the start of the hard work necessary to manage the estate, yet it probably sometimes seems as though there is little energy left. The stresses of the internal dispute, which can still be felt in the community, have also not helped in this respect.

Another drawback from the longevity of the buyout process is that the Pairc community may have missed out on a decade of generous financial incentives for community renewable energy projects. Other communities have been able to take advantage of the opportunities to establish community owned wind turbines which are now generating a flow of income which can sustain other local projects for many years. While it is not yet certain, that era may be at an end as the UK Government reviews the subsidy system for renewable energy.

Of course, it would be wrong to be too pessimistic. After all, the Pairc Trust and the Pairc community were successful. Without the demand by Barry Lomas to share in the income stream from a prospective commercial wind farm, the unusual VAT issue and the mistrust between the two parties, the offer to buy and the conveyancing should have been relatively straightforward. As a result of the delay it is possible for the Trust to learn from the experience of other community landlords, and hopefully follow good practice and learn from mistakes. Having full time paid staff in place has taken much of the load off the volunteer directors. It should be an important aim of the Trust to ensure that paid staff remain a permanent component of the organisation. And the Trust is still held in high regard by most of the funding bodies – although the outlook for public expenditure is generally more difficult.

Community land ownership has taken off in the Outer Hebrides, far more so than anywhere else in Scotland. The majority of the land and population of the Outer Hebrides are now within community owned estates. It is interesting to speculate why. It may be no coincidence that the islands are the heartland of Scotland's crofting and Gaelic communities. Perhaps the island communities were finally waking up to the idea that the islands were being depleted wholesale of their people (especially the young ones) and were in a steep economic and social decline – all requiring radical and direct action that needed to be led by the communities themselves by gaining control of the most important resource of all, the land. It has certainly helped that the local authority has been a strong proponent of community buyouts along all party and non party political lines. Land remains comparatively cheap in the islands and this has also helped, meaning that demand on public funds has been much lower than would have been the case elsewhere. And, once some island communities had bought their land, it was relatively easy for other island communities to communicate and learn from one another compared with many other parts of the Highlands and Islands.

Since taking ownership, the Trust has updated its business plan in consultation with the community and has made a start with projects to promote economic and social development of the area with a view to encouraging local jobs, improving community facilities, and reversing population decline. The challenge is for everyone in the local community to step up to the plate and, with external help, as required, ensure Pairc is a vibrant and thriving place in which to live and work.

The Pairc Trust Since Taking Ownership

(PROVIDED BY THE PAIRC TRUST)

In the five years since eventually gaining legal title to the Pairc Estate in December 2015, the Pairc Trust has taken its first modest but determined steps towards the economic and social regeneration of the area. Our long-term vision is to reverse a century of population decline in South Lochs, by providing additional local jobs, more affordable good housing, and improved community facilities to improve the quality of life for all local residents. Community engagement is central to everything the Trust does, through working groups, social media channels, newsletter articles, an open-door policy for the office, and a series of community events and activities. We work in partnership with other community groups, for example Co-Chomunn na Pairc who own the Ravenspoint Centre in Kershader and which provides the district's only local shop, fuel service, café, museum, and hostel. Our website www.pairctrust.co.uk is an important means of communication and contains up to date information on all current projects and activities.

Unavoidably, progress in the first couple of years after purchase was relatively slow not only because of the need to establish a new office, recruit staff and establish procedures for dealing with day-to-day crofting business on the estate, but also because of issues left over from the buyout process. These included the resolution of the question of whether VAT was chargeable on the purchase price of the estate; and the need to attract additional revenue funding since - because of the unexpected delays in finalising the purchase - some of the award from funding bodies agreed a year or more before the Trust took legal ownership of the estate had already been used prior to December 2015. After lengthy correspondence with HMRC it was established that VAT was chargeable and that the Trust was able to reclaim VAT on eligible expenditure. Additional revenue funding was secured from the Muaitheabhal Community Wind Farm Trust in 2017 to allow Pairc Trust to cover the cost of its staff for a further period, although the number of permanent employees has now been reduced to one. Income is also generated from croft rents, wayleaves, and leases.

Following widespread consultation with the community, the Trust published a Strategic Plan in 2016 which is consistent with the wider strategy for the Western Isles agreed by the main public sector planning partners including Comhairle nan Eilean Siar and Highlands and Islands Enterprise. Working groups on tourism, housing, crofting, and renewable energy were established, drawing on community experience and expertise to target development projects in these areas.

The following projects are now complete or under way:

- Housing. Following a housing needs analysis carried out in 2016 in consultation with the community which confirmed support for additional affordable housing in Pairc, the Trust secured funding to buy and renovate the former care unit in Gravir. A contract to convert the building into two 2-bedroom homes at affordable rents was awarded in 2018 and the first tenants took up residence in August 2019. Other affordable housing projects are being investigated.

- Tourism. A wide-ranging strategy to encourage more visitors to South Lochs has been prepared in consultation with local businesses and residents. This will promote opportunities to experience the area's outstanding natural heritage, history and culture. Improvements to the waymarked Cromore Circular Walk and the Orinsay to Steimreway Walk were carried out in 2018, with new marker posts and a picnic area and information board in Orinsay.

- Development of the estate's assets. A feasibility study of local piers, slipways, and jetties was commissioned in 2018 to identify the needs of existing and future users, and to quantify the potential for increased community benefit. Working with the Crofting Commission, some crofts have been leased to new tenants, including younger people who will help to diversify the age structure of the community. Croft records have been digitised and other improvements made to the Trust's governance arrangements.

- Renewable energy initiatives. A feasibility study into the potential for a pumped storage hydro scheme on the estate near Loch Sgiobacleit was commissioned in 2019. This would be a major long-term project requiring considerable investment but with the potential to generate renewable energy on a large scale and a stream of income for the community over many years.

- Health walks. A series of short community health walks to encourage local people to improve their fitness have been organised by the Trust on Saturdays since 2018. These have proved popular with people of all ages, bringing significant social as well as health benefits.

- Pairc Trust were awarded a grant from the Scottish Land Fund in 2020 to purchase the Resource Centre building in Kershader, adjacent to the Ravenspoint Centre, from Comhairle nan Eilean Siar. This will safeguard the use of this key building by community groups, including the Pairc Playgroup, an exercise room with gym equipment, a community meeting room, and the offices of Pairc Trust and other local organisations.

- To mark the 5th anniversary of the Trust's purchase of the estate, a new bursary scheme is to be introduced in 2021 to support young people from the area in their learning and to bring experience of projects elsewhere back to Pairc.

The Trust is very much aware of the scale of the task ahead, but we are confident that with the support and engagement of the community we can make a real difference to the future of our area and justify the tremendous amount of effort which went into the purchase of the estate for the benefit of the community. As in many other areas, some initiatives had necessarily to be put on hold during the Covid-19 pandemic, and the longer-term repercussions of the virus on economic and social life will need to be assessed, but we look forward to redoubling our efforts on behalf of the Pairc community in the years ahead.

Pairc Trust

January 2021

- APPENDIX ONE -

Scottish Government Decision Letters of March 2011 on the Pairc Trust's Part 3 Applications

(i) 2010 application – eligible croft land

(ii) 2010 application – interest of tenant in tenanted land

(iii) 2005 application

Rural and Environment Directorate
Rural Communities Division

**The Scottish
Government**

T: 0300-244 9754 F: 0300-244 9759
E: Heather.Holmes@scotland.gsi.gov.uk

Mr John Randall
The Pairc Trust Ltd
Ravenspoint
Kershader
Isle of Lewis
HS2 9QA

Your ref/Ur faidhle:
Our ref /Ar faidhle: 2010 croft land
21 March 2011

Dear Mr Randall

**NOTICE BY THE SCOTTISH MINISTERS UNDER SECTION 82 OF THE
LAND REFORM (SCOTLAND) ACT 2003: DECISION ON THE
APPLICATION BY THE PAIRC TRUST LTD FOR CONSENT TO BUY
ELIGIBLE CROFT LAND ETC: APPLICATION DATED 26 FEBRUARY 2010**

Notice under section 82 of the Land Reform (Scotland) Act 2003 ("the Act") is
enclosed.

The Scottish Ministers have considered the application by The Pairc Trust Ltd
("the Trust"), dated 26 February 2010, for consent to buy eligible croft land
etc.

Having considered the criteria in section 74 of the Act and having regard to all
views and responses under section 73(13) of the Act, Ministers have decided
the Trust should proceed with its right to buy the eligible croft land etc on the
Pairc Estate, Isle of Lewis.

The enclosed Notice sets out the reasons for the Minister's decision. Your
attention is drawn to the Notice which provides information about the effect of
the Minister's decision.

In accordance with section 82(1) of the Act, a copy of this letter is being sent
to Mr Barry J Y Lomas, 14 Offchurch Lane, Radford Semele, Leamington
Spa, Warwickshire CV31 1TN, Pairc Crofters Ltd, Anderson Macarthur, Old
Bank of Scotland Buildings, Stornoway HS1, Pairc Renewables Ltd,
Macdonald House, Somerled Square, Portree, Isle of Skye IV51 9EH,
together with all other persons who were invited under section 73(8)(a) to
send views on the application, and the Keeper of the Registers of Scotland.

Yours sincerely

Heather Holmes

Heather Holmes
On behalf of Scottish Ministers

NOTICE UNDER SECTION 82 OF THE LAND REFORM (SCOTLAND) ACT 2003 OF SCOTTISH MINISTERS' DECISION ON AN APPLICATION TO PURCHASE BY A CROFTING COMMUNITY BODY

1. Name of crofting community body.

- The Pairc Trust Ltd

2. Description of eligible croft land, eligible additional land, eligible sporting interests or the interests of the tenant in tenanted land which are the subject of the application.

- The eligible croft and mineral rights applied for are detailed on Map 1, Map 2, and Map 3 which accompanied the application. The eligible croft land etc in the application relates to the townships of: Seaforth Head and Sheildinish, Habost, Kershader, Garyvard, Caverstay, Cromore, Marvig, Calbost, Gravir, Lemreway, and Orinsay.

3. Decision on application and date from which it is effective **(See Notes 1 to 5)**.

- Ministers have decided to consent to the application, dated, 26 February 2010, for the exercise of the right to buy eligible croft land etc. The date on which this decision is effective is 21 March 2011.

4. Any conditions attaching to consent if application is approved.

- None.

5. **Reasons for decision**

Ministers have considered carefully all of the evidence submitted in connection with the application and have had regard to all views and responses under section 73(13) of the Act, and bearing in mind that consent to the application will result in the compulsory purchase of eligible croft land under Part 3 of the Act. Ministers consent to the application as they are satisfied that all of the criteria as set out in section 74 of the Act, are met. In particular:

Section 74(1)(m)

- Ministers are satisfied that, having regard in particular to section 75(1) of the Act, the crofting community have approved the Trust's proposal to exercise the right to buy (section 74(1)(m) of the Act). The Trust has provided sufficient evidence that it undertook a ballot on 10 December 2009 which asked the question "Are you in favour of The Pairc Trust buying the common grazings of the Pairc Estate in Lewis (shown on the plan enclosed with the ballot paper), together with the mineral and sporting rights associated with this land, and the interests of Pairc Renewables Ltd as tenants under the interposed lease granted in their favour by Pairc Crofters Ltd in relation to this land, and for that purpose applying to the Scottish Ministers for consent to buy using the provisions of Part 3 of the Land Reform Act 2003?" The ballot result showed that of the 376 persons eligible to vote, 282 voted. 195 persons voted in favour of the proposal (of which 76 persons were tenants); 87 voted against the proposal and there were no spoilt votes. The Trust complied with the requirement on a Crofting Community Body to submit the ballot result as a precursor to an application indicating that the crofting community support the proposal.

Section 74(1)(i)

- Ministers are satisfied in terms of section 74(1)(i) of the Act that the Trust is a crofting community body which complies with the provisions of section 71 of the Act. In particular, the Trust's Articles of Association comply with the requirements set out in section 71(1) of the Act. Ministers are content that the Articles which were received from the Trust were effective prior to the application from the time when the Trust passed its special resolution at an Extraordinary General Meeting of the Trust on 26 January 2010.

Section 74(1)(j) and (n)

- Ministers are satisfied that the Trust's exercise of the right to buy is compatible with furthering the achievement of sustainable development (section 74(1)(j) of the Act) and is in the public interest (section 74(1)(n) of the Act). This is particularly so bearing in mind the highly remote and fragile nature of the area and the importance of generating greater economic and social opportunity and infrastructure for the community. Ministers are aware of the transformational effect which community acquisition and development of land and other assets can have generally and especially in more remote and fragile areas, such as the Pairc Estate, and how land acquisition also creates prospects for continued growth of, increased confidence within and generally more dynamic and sustainable, communities.

Sustainable development

- In relation specifically to sustainable development (section 74(1)(j) of the Act):

- Ministers are aware that the Trust's application for consent to the exercise of the right to buy the eligible croft land etc is linked to the Trust's separate application for consent to the exercise of the right to buy the interest of the tenant in tenanted land (which also covers the eligible croft land etc). The two applications should therefore be seen in the context of a sustainable plan for the development of the land as a whole. Nevertheless, Ministers have to consider each application on its own merits as required by section 69A of the Act.

- The Trust's application demonstrates that on economic development, its proposals will create employment, will diversify the economic base of the area by introducing new activities (such as additional renewable energy projects, camper-van site, a ranger service for visitors to South Lochs, the development of holiday packages for visitors, the development of a network of paths to explore the Pairc area and other community facilities – though not all of these are associated with the common grazings). The Trust's proposals will help to generate new surplus income in the community which would be available for reinvestment in other projects as defined by the Trust for the benefit of the community, as defined by the Trust. The Trust's acquisition and management of the eligible croft land etc will allow it to develop a number of its key projects and will allow the Pairc community to take the first of a number of steps to acquire and to actively develop and manage the eligible croft land etc and the interest of the tenant in tenanted land (which is the subject of a separate application). The Trust has indicated that both applications are the first stage of a plan to acquire and to actively develop and manage land in the Pairc Estate for the benefit of the community.

- The Trust's application demonstrates that on social sustainability, it has an acceptable level of community support for the project and that there is support for the project beyond the immediate membership of the Trust (see ballot return figure).

- The application shows that the project will directly improve or create specified local services and infrastructure for the benefit of the community as a whole as well as visitors to the area (e.g. social and sustainable housing, a camper van site, a ranger service and holiday packages, paths network and information literature).

- The Trust's application demonstrates that its proposals will provide new amenity for locals and visitors alike in terms of access, (such as a paths network, a ranger service, information literature and information panels at suitable points).

- The Trust's application has the support from relevant public agencies (e.g. Highland and Islands Enterprise (HIE) and Comhairle nan Eilean Siar). The Trust has received substantial funding in recent years from Highlands and Islands Enterprise and has received financial assistance from the Scottish Land Fund in taking forward its plans for a phased community buyout of the Pairc Estate. More generally, HIE is currently supporting the Lochs area of Lewis for enhanced support under the Growth at the Edge / Fas aig an Oir to achieve innovative and sustainable development and that HIE and the LEADER funding programme have co-financed the services of a Local Development Officer who will be managed by the Lochs Community development Group to benefit the whole community. This allows HIE to utilise the full breadth of its powers to work with whole communities, fostering population growth, increased community capacity, economic participation and development of new sustainable revenue streams. The Trust's application also takes account of the opportunities for private sector funding to take forward its proposals arising from development of the land (for example, income from windfarm development). HIE, in its comments on the application, stated that it would consider an application from the Trust towards the acquisition of the land and lease and is committed to working closely with the Trust in the longer term. The Trust has also noted that there are several other possible funding sources which it believes will support them once the purchase price of the Estate is known, and it will be for the Trust to consider those in light of Ministers' consent to this application.

- On financial viability, the Trust has provided a Business Plan which includes a number of proposals together with appropriate costings and revenues estimated over a 10 year period. The Trust had earlier undertaken a feasibility study, dated September 2004, and some of the proposals included have been developed within the Business Plan (such as projects that will bring visitors into the area). The Trust's Business Plan indicates that the Trust has a number of clear aspirations for the land to be purchased and proposals for community benefit (e.g. social housing units, community windfarm, hydro-schemes, camper van site, ranger service, holiday packages, network of paths, boat trips from Kershader and the development of other community facilities at and near Ravenspoint). The Business Plan is largely dependent on the revenues acquired by the proposed community windfarm (and any revenues accrued from the interest of the tenant in tenanted land which the Trust is also seeking to acquire by virtue of a separate application). These revenues appear to provide the finance to allow key projects to be developed and a number of these projects will bring in revenues for the community – such as the sale of house plots, camper van sites, ranger service, holiday packages. Ministers received responses during the public consultation suggesting that the Trust's timescales for the development of the community windfarm were ambitious. Moreover, some of the proposals, will be subject to further statutory consent processes (for example, development of the wind-farm) and may be deliverable over a longer time scale. However, Ministers are satisfied that the Business Plan overall provides sufficient evidence for sustainable development of the land and, in any event, there are a number of key developments for the land which are not dependent on further statutory processes and which, in the shorter term, will generate revenues which can be used by the Trust for the benefit of the community. Ministers also acknowledge that there have been adverse representations made concerning the viability of the Trust's proposals, including that the Trust has used out of date figures and an out of date community appraisal, the figures for national insurance have been incorrectly calculated, that not all costs are attributed to projects (e.g. no staff allocated to the holiday packages, vehicle costs to the ranger service, costs attributed to the guided walks or the sale of houses), there are impractical timescales for projects (such as for renewable energy) and not all the figures are included between the Executive Summary and the Financial Projection Figures. However, Ministers remain satisfied that the Trust's Business Plan as a whole provides sufficient evidence of a viable plan for sustainable development of the land for the benefit of the community.

- Ministers acknowledge that there have been concerns raised as to whether the provision of tourist facilities will attract visitors and be for the benefit of the wider community. The Trust's Feasibility Plan, dated September 2004, together with its Business Plan recognise that tourists could plan an important role in its community development, and that such an opportunity could bring untapped benefits to the community. Ministers recognise that tourism and visitors play an important roles in vitalising fragile communities such as Pairc and have a knock-on effect on local communities in stimulating services and bringing in much-needed revenues.

- Ministers acknowledge that some of the proposals for development in the Business Plan, such as social housing, do not appear to be in accordance with the current local development plan. The planning process and the crofting community right to buy processes are entirely separate matters and are in no way related. The existence of a crofting community right to buy application will not affect Ministers' consideration of any planning matter which may subsequently come before them for determination in terms of the relevant planning legislation. It will be up to the Trust to seek all appropriate planning consents and agreements with the crofters over development on the eligible croft land etc in order to take forward some of its proposals.

- The Trust's application indicates that it's proposals will not have a negative impact on another business or businesses and that it will not duplicate existing provision to a detrimental level (private, community, and public). Its proposals suggest that it will not cause displacement of existing jobs and businesses.

Public interest

- In relation specifically to the public interest (section 74(1)(n)), and having considered this in light of section 74(2) of the Act:

  - Ministers consider that the Trust's proposals will provide lasting benefit to a remote and highly fragile rural community where, hitherto, there have been inadequate social and economic opportunities. In particular, on the basis of the evidence submitted with the application, Ministers are satisfied that the Trust will address issues that affect the local community including:

- the long-term decline and increasing age profile of the local population,
- the shortage of available housing and sites,
- the creation of local services,
- the development of a meaningful income from renewable energy projects,
- wide-ranging proposals to boost tourism which are aimed at bring in more visitors to the area and to create employment, and environmental benefits.

- Ministers believe that the Trust's proposals will provide it with the opportunity to take control of, and develop, the land subject to the right to buy for the direct and lasting benefit of the whole community and will therefore provide it with **greater opportunities** to achieve sustainable development. It will contribute positively to the sustainable development of the land and the 11 townships which form the relevant crofting community, and will deliver a sustainable community as a whole. Ministers believe that there are a number of projects which each have their own income steams that will contribute positively to the community in the short, medium and long terms. Ministers are satisfied that the benefits of the right to buy are not outweighed by any disadvantages to the wider community, the environment or the economy and are not disproportionate to the degree of any harm to private interests.

- Ministers acknowledge that, notwithstanding general community support for the right to buy as evidenced by the ballot, a number of representations have been made about the Trust's organisational and management controls in how it has been managed and works with and relates to the community, and that the Trust will have to work hard to overcome these if it is to become a community landowner. While Ministers accept that there have been criticisms, the Trust has stated that it has taken steps to deal with them (including the provision of information to the community and to increasing dialogue with other community organisations in the Pairc area).

- Ministers also acknowledge that representations have been received which ask whether the Trust is acting in the interests of the community as a whole. The Trust has provided evidence that its motivation is to promote sustainable development in all parts of the community in line with local priorities. The Trust already has close links with the grazings committees of the townships and recognises the rights of the crofting tenants under the interest of the tenant in tenanted land. Ministers are satisfied that the Trust has an awareness of the needs of the different sections of the community and that it needs to represent the community as a whole.

NOTES

1.   If the transfer of the land/tenanted land is not completed within 6 months, or within 2 months of the price being fixed, the application is treated as being withdrawn.

2.   A decision of the Scottish Ministers to consent to an application relating to land/tenanted land may be appealed by summary application to the Sheriff by the following persons—

(a) any person who is a member of the crofting community defined in relation to the applicant crofting community in pursuance of section 71 of the Act;

(b) the owner of or, as the case may be, person entitled to the subjects of the application;

(c) any other person who has any interest in the land or eligible sporting interests giving rise to a right which is legally enforceable by that person;

(d) the owners of all land contiguous to land which consists of the subjects of the application;

(e) the Crofters Commission; and

(f) any other person whom the Scottish Ministers considered to have an interest in the application under section 73(8)(a) of the Act.

3.   A decision of the Scottish Ministers to refuse an application may be appealed by summary application to the Sheriff by the applicant crofting community body.

4.   A decision of the Scottish Ministers to consent to an application has the following consequences—

(a) the Scottish Ministers must within 7 days appoint a valuer of the croft land to be acquired;

(b) the owner of the croft land/tenanted land is required to make available to the crofting community body the title deeds of the land to be acquired/lease relating to the tenanted land within 6 weeks of the consent by the Scottish Ministers;

(c) in the event that the application relating to land proposed that there could be a leaseback of the eligible sporting interests to the owner, the current owner has notified the Scottish Ministers that he wishes a lease back and the Scottish Ministers have not been provided with a copy of an agreement on the terms and conditions of the lease then, within 7 days, the Scottish Ministers will refer the question of what terms and conditions are appropriate to the Land Court so that the Court may determine these terms and conditions;

(d) any rights of pre-emption, redemption or reversion or deriving from any option to purchase are suspended as from the date of the Scottish Ministers' approval and are revived either when the transfer of the land is completed, or if such a transfer is not completed, because the crofting community body does not proceed with the purchase.

5.   A copy of the Scottish Ministers' decision—

(a) must be lodged in the Register of Crofting Community Rights to Buy to be held by the Crofters Commission and will be available for public inspection;

(b) must be sent to—

(i) the owner of the land, or as the case may be, the person entitled to the eligible sporting interests, or the tenant to which the application relates;

(ii) every other person whom Ministers invited to give views on the application;

(iii) in the case of a decision to consent to the application, to the Keeper of the Registers of Scotland.

Rural and Environment Directorate
Rural Communities Division

The Scottish Government

T: 0300-244 9754 F: 0300-244 9759
E: Heather.Holmes@scotland.gsi.gov.uk

Mr John Randall
The Pairc Trust Ltd
Ravenspoint
Kershader
Isle of Lewis
HS2 9QA

Your ref/Ur faidhle:
Our ref /Ar faidhle: 2010 interest of the tenant

21 March 2011

Dear Mr Randall

NOTICE BY THE SCOTTISH MINISTERS UNDER SECTION 82 OF THE LAND REFORM (SCOTLAND) ACT 2003: DECISION ON THE APPLICATION BY THE PAIRC TRUST LTD FOR CONSENT TO BUY THE INTEREST OF THE TENANT IN TENANTED LAND: APPLICATION DATED 26 FEBRUARY 2010

Notice under section 82 of the Land Reform (Scotland) Act 2003 ("the Act") is enclosed.

The Scottish Ministers have considered the application by The Pairc Trust Ltd ("the Trust"), dated 26 February 2010 for consent to buy the interest of the tenant in tenanted land.

Having considered the terms of sections 73 and 74 Ministers have decided the Trust should proceed with its right to buy the interest of the tenant in tenanted land over the eligible croft land etc on the Pairc Estate, Isle of Lewis.

The enclosed Notice sets out the reasons for the Minister's decision. Your attention is drawn to the Notes which provide information about the effect of the Minister's decision.

In accordance with section 82(1) of the Act, a copy of this letter is being sent to Mr Barry J Y Lomas, 14 Offchurch Lane, Radford Semele, Leamington Spa, Warwickshire CV31 1TN, Pairc Crofters Ltd, Anderson Macarthur, Old Bank of Scotland Buildings, Stornoway HS1, Pairc Renewables Ltd, Macdonald House, Somerled Square, Portree, Isle of Skye IV51 9EH, together with all other persons who were invited under section 73(8)(a) to send views on the application, and the Keeper of the Registers of Scotland.

Yours sincerely

Heather Holmes

Heather Holmes
On behalf of Scottish Ministers

NOTICE UNDER SECTION 82 OF THE LAND REFORM (SCOTLAND) ACT 2003 OF SCOTTISH MINISTERS' DECISION ON AN APPLICATION TO PURCHASE BY A CROFTING COMMUNITY BODY

1. Name of crofting community body.

- The Pairc Trust Ltd

2. Description of eligible croft land, eligible additional land, eligible sporting interests or the interests of the tenant in tenanted land which are the subject of the application.

- The interest of the tenant in tenanted land applied for is detailed on Map 1, Map 2, and Map 3 which accompanied the Trust's application. The interest of the tenant in tenanted land covers the eligible croft land etc relating to the townships of: Seaforth Head and Sheildinish, Habost, Kershader, Garyvard, Caverstay, Cromore, Marvig, Calbost, Gravir, Lemreway, and Orinsay.

3. Decision on application and date from which it is effective **(See Notes 1 to 5)**.

- Ministers have decided to consent to the application dated 26 February 2010 for the exercise of the right to buy the interest of the tenant in tenanted land. The date on which this decision is effective is 21 March 2011.

4. Any conditions attaching to consent if application is approved.

- None.

5. **Reasons for decision**

Ministers have considered carefully all of the evidence submitted in connection with the application and have had regard to all views and responses under section 73(13) of the Act, and bearing in mind that consent to the application will result in the compulsory purchase of the interests of the tenant in tenanted land under Part 3 of the Act. Ministers consent to the application as they are satisfied that all of the criteria as set out in section 74 of the Act, are met. In particular:

Section 74(1)(m)

- Ministers are satisfied that, having regard in particular to section 75(1) of the Act, the crofting community have approved the Trust's proposal to exercise the right to buy (section 74(1)(m) of the Act). The Trust has provided sufficient evidence that it undertook a ballot on 10 December

2009 which asked the question "Are you in favour of The Pairc Trust buying the common grazings of the Pairc Estate in Lewis (shown on the plan enclosed with the ballot paper), together with the mineral and sporting rights associated with this land, and the interests of Pairc Renewables Ltd as tenants under the interposed lease granted in their favour by Pairc Crofters Ltd in relation to this land, and for that purpose applying to the Scottish Ministers for consent to buy using the provisions of Part 3 of the Land Reform Act 2003?" The ballot result showed that of the 376 persons eligible to vote, 282 voted. 195 persons voted in favour of the proposal (of which 76 persons were tenants); 87 voted against the proposal and there were no spoilt votes. The Trust complied with the requirement on a Crofting Community Body to submit the ballot result as a precursor to an application indicating that the crofting community support the proposal.

Section 74(1)(i)

- Ministers are satisfied in terms of section 74(1)(i) of the Act that the Trust is a crofting community body which complies with the provisions of section 71 of the Act. In particular, the Trust's Articles of Association comply with the requirements set out in section 71(1) of the Act. Ministers are content that the Articles which were received from the Trust were effective prior to the application from the time when the Trust passed its special resolution at an Extraordinary General Meeting of the Trust on 26 January 2010.

Section 74(1)(j) and (n)

- Ministers are satisfied that the Trust's exercise of the right to buy is compatible with furthering the achievement of sustainable development (section 74(1)(j) of the Act) and is in the public interest (section 74(1)(n) of the Act). This is particularly so bearing in mind the highly remote and fragile nature of the area and the importance of generating greater economic and social opportunity and infrastructure for the community. Ministers are aware of the transformational effect which community acquisition and development of land and other assets can have in fragile areas, such as the Pairc Estate, and how they can help create continued growth of rural communities, more dynamic and sustainable communities, together with communities that have increased confidence.

Sustainable development

- In relation specifically to sustainable development (section 74(1)(j) of the Act):

- Ministers are aware that the Trust's application for consent to the exercise of the right to buy the interest of the tenant in tenanted lend ("the interest") is linked to the Trust's separate application for consent to the exercise of the right to buy the eligible croft land etc (which that interest also covers). The two applications should therefore be seen in the context of a sustainable plan for the development of the land as a whole. Nevertheless, Ministers have to consider each application on its own merits as required by section 69A of the Act.

- The Trust's application demonstrates that it will diversify the economic base of the area by introducing new activities. The acquisition of the interest includes land which forms part of the proposed Pairc commercial windfarm (the consent for which is the subject of a separate statutory process) which relates to 14 of the 26 turbines located over the common grazings of the Pairc Estate, the development of an extensive commercial windfarm and any revenues associated with these turbines. The acquisition of the interest will enable the Trust to negotiate with Scottish and Southern Energy (the sub-tenants under a sub-lease of the interest and the Developer for the proposed Pairc commercial wind farm ("the Developer")) to amend the extent of the geographical area covered by the sub-lease in order to exclude all areas not included in the current Pairc commercial wind-farm proposal. The Trust would then have powers to carry out its developments on the eligible croft land generally (as proposed in its separate application for consent) without the requirement to refer any of its proposals to a landlord or tenant. This will *inter alia* allow the Trust to create employment, diversify the economic base of the area by introducing new activities (such as additional renewable energy projects of a 2 turbine community wind farm, camper-van site, a ranger service for visitors to South Lochs, the development of holiday packages for visitors, the development of a network of paths to explore the Pairc area and other community facilities). These proposed activities are set out in the Trust's Business Plan which is similar for both its applications though there is a separate Annex 4 specifically concerning the proposed use, development and management of the interest. The Trust's proposals will help to generate new surplus income in the community which would be available for reinvestment in other projects and for the benefit of the community, as defined by the Trust.

- The Trust's proposals will help to generate new surplus income in the community which would be available for reinvestment in other projects as defined by the Trust for the benefit of the community. Should planning consent be granted for the proposed Pairc commercial windfarm, and that windfarm be developed, the acquisition of the interest will provide opportunities for substantial income to the crofters, the community and the landowner (who will retain the interest of the tenant on the in-bye land on the Pairc Estate and the land at Steimreway in the south-west of the Pairc Estate) for several generations. The Trust's acquisition and management of the interest will allow it to develop a number of its key projects and will allow the Pairc community to take the first of a number of steps to acquire and to actively develop and manage the eligible croft land etc (which is the subject of a separate application). The Trust has indicated that both applications are the first stage of a plan to acquire and to actively develop and manage land in the Pairc Estate for the benefit of the community.

- The Trust's application demonstrates that on social sustainability, it has an acceptable level of community support for the project and that there is support for the project beyond the immediate membership of The Pairc Trust (see ballot return figure).

- The Trust's application shows that the acquisition of the interest will, subject to negotiations with the Developer and other existing rights holders, also enable the Trust to, *inter alia*, directly improve or create specified local services and infrastructure for the benefit of the community as a whole as well as visitors to the area (e.g. social and sustainable housing, a camper van site, a ranger service and holiday packages, paths network and information literature), as well as local amenity for visitors alike in terms of access (such as a paths network, a ranger service, information literature and information panels at suitable points.

- Whilst, as acknowledged by the Trust in its application, the timing of any community benefit arising from the Pairc commercial windfarm is "at present uncertain" as consent for that project has still to be granted, Ministers are satisfied that in the longer-term the Trust's proposals have the potential to bring significant revenues to the Trust and to the community (as also the landowner in the interest of the tenant that is not being acquired by the Trust) and to enable the Trust to bring in revenue steams from other projects for the benefit of the community.

- The Trust's application has the support from relevant public agencies (e.g. Highland and Islands Enterprise and Comhairle nan Eilean Siar). The Trust has received substantial funding in recent years from Highlands and Islands Enterprise (HIE) and has received financial assistance from the Scottish Land Fund in taking forward its plans for a phased community buyout of the Pairc Estate. More generally, HIE is currently supporting the Lochs area of Lewis for enhanced support under the Growth at the Edge / Fas aig an Oir to achieve innovative and sustainable development and that HIE and the LEADER funding programme have co-financed the services of a Local Development Officer who will be managed by the Lochs Community development Group to benefit the whole community. This allows HIE to utilise the full breadth of its powers to work with whole communities, fostering population growth, increased community capacity, economic participation and development of new sustainable revenue streams. The Trust's application also takes account of the opportunities for private sector funding to take forward its proposals arising from development of the land (for example, income from windfarm development). HIE, in its comments on the application stated that it would consider an application from the Trust towards the acquisition of the land and lease and is committed to working closely with The Pairc

Trust in the longer term. The Trust has also noted that there are several funding sources which it believes will support them once the purchase price of the interest of the tenant is known, and it will be for the Trust to consider those in light of the Minister's consent to this application.

- On financial viability, the Trust has provided a Business Plan which includes a number of proposals together with appropriate costings and revenues estimated over a 10 year period. This includes figures for the interest together with windfarm community benefit money from the proposed Pairc commercial windfarm and a separate proposed community windfarm. The Trust had earlier undertaken a feasibility study, dated September 2004, and some of the proposals included have been developed within the Business Plan (e.g. projects that will bring visitors into the area and renewables (e.g. wind turbines as a community owned scheme, small scale hydro, and wave/tidal). The Trust's Business Plan indicates that the Trust has a number of clear aspirations which it wishes to achieve and which it considers that the interest of the tenant in tenanted land will facilitate that development (e.g. social housing units, community windfarm, hydro-schemes, camper van site, the network of paths, and generation of community benefit money). The Business Plan is largely dependent on the revenues acquired by the proposed community windfarm and the Pairc commercial windfarm, both of which will be achieved through the acquisition of the interest. These revenues appear to provide the finance to allow key projects to be developed (a number of other projects will also bring in revenues for the community – such as the sale of house plots, camper van sites, ranger service, holiday packages). Ministers acknowledge that responses to the application suggest that the Trust's timescales for the development of the community windfarm are ambitious and that some of the proposals will be subject to further statutory consent processes (e.g. development of both of the commercial and the community windfarms) and so may therefore be deliverable over a longer time scale. However, Ministers are satisfied that the Business Plan overall provides sufficient evidence for sustainable development of the interest and, in any event, the acquisition of the interest is not of itself dependent on further statutory processes and will, even over the shorter term, generate revenues which can be used by the Trust for the benefit of the community.

- Ministers also acknowledge that there have been further adverse representations made concerning the viability of the Trust's proposals (the Trust submitted the same Business Plan in respect of its two applications), including that the Trust has used out of date figures and an out of date community appraisal, the figures for national insurance have been incorrectly calculated, that not all costs are attributed to projects (e.g. no staff allocated to the holiday packages, vehicle costs to the ranger service, costs attributed to the guided walks or the sale of houses), there are impractical timescales for projects (such as for renewable energy) and not all the figures are included between the

Executive Summary and the Financial Projection Figures. However, Ministers remain satisfied that the Trust's Business Plan overall provides sufficient evidence of a viable plan for the sustainable development of the interest for the benefit of the community and that the acquisition of the interest will facilitate wider developments on the eligible croft land etc which the Trust is seeking to acquire through its separate application.

- The Trust's application indicates that it's proposals will not have a negative impact on another business or businesses and that it will not duplicate existing provision to a detrimental level (private, community, and public). Its proposals suggest that it will not cause displacement of existing jobs and businesses.

Public interest

- In relation specifically to the public interest (section 74(1)(n)), and having considered this in light of section 74(2) of the Act:

  - Ministers consider that the Trust's proposals will provide lasting benefit to a remote and highly fragile rural community where, hitherto, there have been inadequate social and economic opportunities. In particular, on the basis of the evidence submitted with the application, Ministers are satisfied that they will address issues relating to the management of the eligible croft land etc which is being acquired by the Trust by virtue of another application and the local community including:

    - It will give the Trust the opportunity to amend the lease by mutual consent to facilitate greater benefit for the Pairc community through the acquisition of community benefit from 14 of the 26 turbines of the proposed Pairc commercial windfarm and the proposed community windfarm.

    - It will allow the Trust to facilitate the development of a number of developments on the eligible croft land etc which the Trust is also seeking to acquire through a separate application. This will allow the Trust to develop projects such as social housing, hydro schemes, a community windfam, a camper van site, a network of paths to explore the Pairc area).

    - Through these activities, the Trust will be able to address the following:

      - the long-term decline and increasing age profile of the local population.
      - the shortage of available housing and sites.
      - the creation of local services.
      - the development of a meaningful income from renewable energy projects.

- wide-ranging proposals to boost tourism which are aimed at bring in more visitors to the area and to create employment, and environmental benefits.

- Ministers consider that the Trust's proposals will provide it with the opportunity to take control of, and develop, the interest and, by virtue of the separate application, the eligible croft land etc for the direct and lasting benefit of the whole community and will therefore provide it with **greater opportunities** overall to achieve sustainable development. It will contribute positively to the sustainable development of the interest of the tenant (and to the eligible croft land etc) and the 11 townships which form the relevant crofting community, and will deliver a sustainable community as a whole. Ministers consider that the acquisition of the interest of the tenant in tenanted land will facilitate a number of projects which each have their own income steams which will contribute positively to the community in the short, medium and long term.

- Ministers are therefore satisfied that the benefits of the right to buy are not outweighed by any disadvantages to the wider community, the environment or the economy and are not disproportionate to the degree of any harm to private interests.

- Ministers acknowledge that, notwithstanding general support for the right to buy as evidenced by the ballot, a number of representations have been made about the Trust's organisational and management controls in how it has been managed and works with and relates to the community, and that the Trust will have to work hard to overcome these if it is to become a community landowner. While Ministers accept that there have been criticisms, the Trust has stated that it has taken steps to deal with them (including the provision of information to the community and to increasing dialogue with other community organisations in the Pairc area).

- Ministers also acknowledge that representations have been received which ask whether the Trust is acting in the interests of the community as a whole. The Trust has provided evidence that its motivation is to promote sustainable development in all parts of the community in line with local priorities. The Trust already has close links with the grazings committees of the townships and recognises the rights of the crofting tenants under the interest of the tenant in tenanted land. Ministers are satisfied that the Trust has an awareness of the needs of the different sections of the community and that it needs to represent the community as a whole.

NOTES

1. If the transfer of the land/tenanted land is not completed within 6 months, or within 2 months of the price being fixed, the application is treated as being withdrawn.

2. A decision of the Scottish Ministers to consent to an application relating to land/tenanted land may be appealed by summary application to the Sheriff by the following persons—

    (a) any person who is a member of the crofting community defined in relation to the applicant crofting community in pursuance of section 71 of the Act;

    (b) the owner of or, as the case may be, person entitled to the subjects of the application;

    (c) any other person who has any interest in the land or eligible sporting interests giving rise to a right which is legally enforceable by that person;

    (d) the owners of all land contiguous to land which consists of the subjects of the application;

    (e) the Crofters Commission; and

    (f) any other person whom the Scottish Ministers considered to have an interest in the application under section 73(8)(a) of the Act.

3. A decision of the Scottish Ministers to refuse an application may be appealed by summary application to the Sheriff by the applicant crofting community body.

4. A decision of the Scottish Ministers to consent to an application has the following consequences—
    (a) the Scottish Ministers must within 7 days appoint a valuer of the croft land to be acquired;

    (b) the owner of the croft land/tenanted land is required to make available to the crofting community body the title deeds of the land to be acquired/lease relating to the tenanted land within 6 weeks of the consent by the Scottish Ministers;

    (c) in the event that the application relating to land proposed that there could be a leaseback of the eligible sporting interests to the owner, the current owner has notified the Scottish Ministers that he wishes a lease back and the Scottish Ministers have not been provided with a copy of an agreement on the terms and conditions of the lease then, within 7 days, the Scottish Ministers will refer the question of what terms and conditions are appropriate to the Land Court so that the Court may determine these terms and conditions;

    (d) any rights of pre-emption, redemption or reversion or deriving from any option to purchase are suspended as from the date of the Scottish Ministers' approval and are revived either when the transfer of the land is completed, or if such a transfer is not completed, because the crofting community body does not proceed with the purchase.

5. A copy of the Scottish Ministers' decision—

    (a) must be lodged in the Register of Crofting Community Rights to Buy to be held by the Crofters Commission and will be available for public inspection;

    (b) must be sent to—

        (i) the owner of the land, or as the case may be, the person entitled to the eligible sporting interests, or the tenant to which the application relates;

        (ii) every other person whom Ministers invited to give views on the application;

        (iii) in the case of a decision to consent to the application, to the Keeper of the Registers of Scotland.

Rural and Environment Directorate
Rural Communities Division

The Scottish
Government

T: 0300-244 9754 F: 0300-244 9759
E: Heather.Holmes@scotland.gsi.gov.uk

Mr John Randall
The Pairc Trust Ltd
Ravenspoint
Kershader
Isle of Lewis
HS2 9QA

Your ref/Ur faidhle:
Our ref /Ar faidhle: 2005 application
21 March 2011

Dear Mr Randall

NOTICE BY THE SCOTTISH MINISTERS UNDER SECTION 82 OF THE LAND REFORM (SCOTLAND) ACT 2003: DECISION ON THE APPLICATION BY THE PAIRC TRUST LTD   FOR CONSENT TO BUY ELIGIBLE CROFT LAND ETC: APPLICATION DATED 20 MAY 2005

Notice under section 82 of the Land Reform (Scotland) Act 2003 ("the Act") is enclosed.

The Scottish Ministers have considered the application by The Pairc Trust Ltd, dated 20 May 2005, for consent to buy eligible croft land etc.

Having considered the criteria in section 74 of the Act and having regard to all views and responses under section 73(13) of the Act, Ministers have decided The Pairc Trust Ltd should not proceed with its right to buy the eligible croft land etc on the Pairc Estate, Isle of Lewis.

The enclosed Notice sets out the reasons for the Minister's decision. Your attention is drawn to the Notes which provide information about the effect of the Minister's decision and on rights of appeal against the decision by Scottish Ministers.

In accordance with section 82(1) of the Act, a copy of this letter is being sent to Mr Barry J Y Lomas, 14 Offchurch Lane, Radford Semele, Leamington Spa, Warwickshire CV31 1TN, Pairc Crofters Ltd, Anderson Macarthur, Old Bank of Scotland Buildings, Stornoway HS1, Pairc Renewables Ltd, Macdonald House, Somerled Square, Portree, Isle of Skye IV51 9EH, together with all the persons who were invited under section 73(8)(a) to send views on the application.

Yours sincerely

Heather Holmes
On behalf of Scottish Ministers

NOTICE UNDER SECTION 82 OF THE LAND REFORM (SCOTLAND) ACT 2003 OF SCOTTISH MINISTERS' DECISION ON AN APPLICATION TO PURCHASE BY A CROFTING COMMUNITY BODY

1. Name of crofting community body.

   • The Pairc Trust Ltd

2. Description of eligible croft land, eligible additional land, eligible sporting interests or the interests of the tenant in tenanted land which are the subject of the application.

   • The eligible croft land and sporting interests applied for are detailed on Map 1, Map 2, and Map 3 which accompanied the application. The eligible croft land etc in the application relates to the townships of: Seaforth Head, Sheildinish, Habost, Kershader, Garyvard, Caverstay, Cromore, Marvig, Calbost, Gravir, Lemreway, and Orinsay.

3. Decision on application and date from which it is effective **(See Notes 1 to 5)**.

   • Ministers have decided to reject the application, dated 20 May 2005, for the right to buy eligible croft land etc. The date on which this decision is effective is 21 March 2011.

4. Any conditions attaching to consent if application is approved.

   • Not applicable. The application has been rejected.

5. **Reasons for decision.**

   Ministers have considered carefully all of the evidence submitted in connection with the application and have had regard to all views and responses under section 73(13) of the Act, and bearing in mind that consent of the application will result in the compulsory purchase of the eligible croft land etc under Part 3 of the Act. The application dated 20 May 2005 has been rejected for the following reasons:

   Sustainable development

   In terms of section 74(1)(j) Ministers are not satisfied that The Pairc Trust's exercise of the right to buy under Part 3 of the Act is compatible with furthering the achievement of sustainable development.

   • The proposed activities largely include activities that are currently undertaken by the present landowner, Pairc Crofters

Ltd, and the holder of the shooting lease and seek to benefit these parties. They do not provide any significant additional activities that could be developed by a community landowner for its community and its community benefit.

- The Trust's Business Plan is generalised, lacks detail, is based on a number of assumptions, and does not provide any clear benefit for the "community" as defined by the Trust; neither does it show how ownership of the common grazings would make a real difference to that "community". Ministers do not believe that funders would look upon the Trust's Business Plan favourably when considering whether to provide the Trust with financial assistance to buy out the common grazings etc for the community.

- The Trust's Business Plan includes limited income generating opportunities; the amount of income that will be generated will not provide significant benefit to the Trust's defined "community".

- While Ministers are aware of the impact of the interest of the tenant on the common grazings (and these have been pointed out by both the Trust and the landowner), they are not satisfied that having looked at the Trust's proposals, before considering the impact of the impact of the interest of the tenant on tenanted land, that they are compatible with furthering the achievement of sustainable development.

Public interest

In terms of 74(1)(n) of the Act, and having considered this in light of section 74(2) of the Act, Ministers are not satisfied that it is in the public interest that the right to buy should be exercised.

- The Trust has not provided any clear evidence of how the acquisition of the common grazings etc would provide benefits on a short, medium or long term to the "community" as defined by the Trust or to the 12 townships.

- The proposed activities largely include activities that are currently undertaken by the present landowner, Pairc Crofters Ltd, and the holder of the shooting lease and seek to benefit these parties. They do not provide any significant additional activities that could be developed by a community landowner for its community and its community benefit.

- Since the Trust submitted its application for consent for croft land etc, dated 20 May 2005, it has submitted a further application for the eligible croft land etc, dated 26 February 2010, which reflects the up-to-date proposals for essentially the same area of land. Although the Trust has not formally withdrawn its application, Ministers consider that it has, in effect, been superseded by the application of 26 February 2010, which Ministers are considering separately.

NOTES

1. If the transfer of the land/tenanted land is not completed within 6 months, or within 2 months of the price being fixed, the application is treated as being withdrawn.

2. A decision of the Scottish Ministers to consent to an application relating to land/tenanted land may be appealed by summary application to the Sheriff by the following persons–

    (a) any person who is a member of the crofting community defined in relation to the applicant crofting community in pursuance of section 71 of the Act;

    (b) the owner of or, as the case may be, person entitled to the subjects of the application;

    (c) any other person who has any interest in the land or eligible sporting interests giving rise to a right which is legally enforceable by that person;

    (d) the owners of all land contiguous to land which consists of the subjects of the application;

    (e) the Crofters Commission; and

    (f) any other person whom the Scottish Ministers considered to have an interest in the application under section 73(8)(a) of the Act.

3. A decision of the Scottish Ministers to refuse an application may be appealed by summary application to the Sheriff by the applicant crofting community body.

4. A decision of the Scottish Ministers to consent to an application has the following consequences–
    (a) the Scottish Ministers must within 7 days appoint a valuer of the croft land to be acquired;

    (b) the owner of the croft land/tenanted land is required to make available to the crofting community body the title deeds of the land to be acquired/lease relating to the tenanted land within 6 weeks of the consent by the Scottish Ministers;

    (c) in the event that the application relating to land proposed that there could be a leaseback of the eligible sporting interests to the owner, the current owner has notified the Scottish Ministers that he wishes a lease back and the Scottish Ministers have not been provided with a copy of an agreement on the terms and conditions of the lease then, within 7 days, the Scottish Ministers will refer the question of what terms and conditions are appropriate to the Land Court so that the Court may determine these terms and conditions;

    (d) any rights of pre-emption, redemption or reversion or deriving from any option to purchase are suspended as from the date of the Scottish Ministers' approval and are revived either when the transfer of the land is completed, or if such a transfer is not completed, because the crofting community body does not proceed with the purchase.

5.   A copy of the Scottish Ministers' decision–

(a) must be lodged in the Register of Crofting Community Rights to Buy to be held by the Crofters Commission and will be available for public inspection;

(b) must be sent to–

(i) the owner of the land, or as the case may be, the person entitled to the eligible sporting interests, or the tenant to which the application relates;

(ii) every other person whom Ministers invited to give views on the application;

(iii) in the case of a decision to consent to the application, to the Keeper of the Registers of Scotland.

- APPENDIX TWO -

Directors of the Pairc Trust 2004 – 2015 (PROVIDED BY THE PAIRC TRUST)

Alston, Alison (2004 – 2008)

Begg, Ian (2009 – 2011)

Black, Morris (2004 – 2011)

Campbell, Maretta (2011 – 2015)

Fardoe, Keith (2009)

Hollis, Tim (2015)

Kennedy, Ken (2006 – 2009)

Macarthur, Donald (2004 – 2015)

Macdonald, Donnie (2002 – 2016) (chairman 2004 – 2009)

Macdonald, Finlay (2004 – 2009)

Mackay, Angus (2004 – 2006)

Mackay, Donald (2004 – 2007)

Mackenzie, Roddy (2004 – 2005)

Mackinnon, Angus (2004 – 2009)

Maclennan, DM (2006 – 2009) (chairman 2009)

Macleod, Donald (2005 – 2008)

Macleod, Norrie (2009 – 2012)

Macmillan, Neil (2005 – 2006)

McDowall, Angus (2004 – 2015) (chairman 2009 – 2015)

McLaughlin, Jim (2010 – 2015)

Morrison, Anne (2010 – 2014)

Mortimore, Steve – (2008 – 2012, 2014 – 2015)

Randall, John (2008 – 2015)

Wilson, Alan (2011 – 2015)

- BIBLIOGRAPHY -

OVERVIEW

Much of the material on which this book is based has been derived from the Pairc Trust – both in writing and orally – and from official sources such as Scottish Government, the Scottish Land Court and the National Records of Scotland.

In addition, there is a wealth of additional 'secondary' information that has been drawn on by the author – though by no means do most of these deal directly with the Pairc Estate *per se.* These sources include books, articles, pamphlets, newspapers, Parliamentary Papers and reports by public bodies. They provide important background and historical information about Pairc, South Lochs, the island of Lewis and the Outer Hebrides. These additional sources comprise useful background reading material for the general reader of this book. But importantly, they help to put the Pairc Estate and the community buyout into a much wider geographical, historical, political and social context.

In the author's view the most valuable (and interesting) of these are the following books:

- James Hunter, *From the Low Tide of the Sea to the Highest Mountain Tops* (published 2012);

- James Hunter, *The Making of the Crofting Community* (first published 1976);

- James Hunter, *The Claim of Crofting: The Scottish Highlands and Islands 1930 – 1990* (published 1991);

- Ewen Cameron, *Land for the People? The British Government and the Scottish Highlands, 1880 – 1925* (published 1996);

- Leah Leneman, *Fit for Heroes? Land Settlement in Scotland After World War I* (published 1989);

- Iain Robertson, *Landscapes of Protest in the Scottish Highlands After 1914: The Later Highland Wars* (published 2013).

In addition, the Pairc Historical Society (Comunn Eachdraidh na Pairc) has published a large number of books and booklets covering a multitude of subjects about the local area – too numerous to mention here. Anyone with an interest in the area should refer to the Society's website www.cepairc.com

The author has found the series dealing with the history of each
of the area's crofting townships of immense interest and help.
Similarly, the Islands Book Trust has also produced numerous
relevant and interesting publications. These too are best referred to
on the Trust's own website www.islandsbooktrust.org.

BOOKS

The most useful book on community land ownership in the
Highlands and Islands is, undoubtedly in the author's opinion,
Jim Hunter's *From the Low Tide of the Sea to the Highest Mountain
Tops*. This reviews and summarises the generally positive recent
experience of community landowning groups up until the date of
publication.

In terms of providing a historical context to crofting and land
settlement in the Highlands and Islands, although first published
in 1976, now well over forty years ago, it is remarkable how Jim
Hunter's *The Making of the Crofting Community* remains so fresh,
comprehensive and up-to-date in its analysis and views. It has
stood the test of time exceedingly well and has been an invaluable
reference source for the author for writing this and other books. It is
a testament to the quality of *The Making of the Crofting Community*
and its author, that Jim Hunter has had the opportunity (twice) to
add a new preface and postscript to what has been an otherwise
unaltered script. Hopefully the same sort of opportunity might be
afforded, in time, to Ewen Cameron, for his excellent text. Sadly,
Leah Leneman died in 1999 and so the same opportunities will not
be available for *Fit for Heroes?*

A number of books cover various aspects of community land
ownership in the Highlands and Islands. These are listed below. Of
particular interest in relation to the Pairc Estate community buyout
are John MacAskill's *We Have Won the Land*; and Janet Hunter's *A
Future for North Harris*.

Adam, Robert, M, *Footfall in Lewis: Cas – Cheum An Leòdhas* (Isle of
Lewis, 2006).

Armstrong, A. M., & Mather, A. S., *Land Ownership and Land Use in
the Scottish Highlands* (Aberdeen, 1983).

Buchanan, Joni, *The Lewis Land Struggle – Na Gaisgich* (Isle of
Lewis, 1996).

Burnett, John, *The Making of the Modern Scottish Highlands 1939 – 1965* (Dublin, 2011).

Caird, J. B., *Park, A Geographical Study of a Lewis Crofting District* (1958).

Cameron, Ewen A., *Land for the People? The British Government and the Scottish Highlands, c. 1880 – 1925* (East Linton, 1996).

Cameron, Ewen A., *Impaled Upon a Thistle, Scotland since 1880* (Edinburgh, 2010).

Cameron, Ewen A., (editor), *Recovering from the Clearances – Land Struggle, Resettlement and Community Ownership in the Hebrides* (Isle of Lewis, 2013).

Chambers, Bob, *For Want of Land: Hebridean Croft Schemes of the 1920s and 1930s* (Hexham, 2016).

Chambers, Bob, *The Creation of Crofting Schemes in Uig Parish on the Isle of Lewis* (Hexham, 2016).

Chambers, Bob, *Over the Sea to Skye: North Talisker and Other Skye Crofting Schemes* (Hexham, 2017).

Chambers, Bob, *Twentieth – century Crofting Schemes on Tiree and Coll* (Hexham, 2016).

Chambers, Bob, *Solving the Lewis Land Problem: The Contribution of Fishermen – Cottar Schemes* (Hexham, 2017).

Chambers, Bob, *Off the Beaten Track: The Role of Roads and other Infrastructure in the Life or Death of Remote Hebridean Communities of the 1920s and 1930s* (Hexham, 2018).

Chambers, Bob, *Gaining Back the Ground: Publicly Funded Land Initiatives in Harris since the Clearances* (Hexham, 2020).

Chambers, Bob, *All Built to the Same Pattern: Croft House Designs in the Hebrides* (Hexham, 2020).

Collier, Adam, *The Crofting Problem* (Cambridge, 1953).

Comunn Eachdraidh Cheann a' Loch, *Gleanings* (Stornoway, 1997).

Cragoe, Matthew, & Readman, Paul, (editors), *The Land Question in Britain, 1750 – 1950* (Basingstoke, 2010).

Cramb, Auslan, *Who Owns Scotland Now? The Use and Abuse of Private Land* (Edinburgh, 2000, first published 1996).

Crofters Commission, *Crofting, People and Politics: Five Decades of the Crofters Commission* (Argyll, 2005).

Devine, T. M., *The Great Highland Famine: Hunger, Emigration and the Scottish Highlands in the Nineteenth Century* (Edinburgh, 2004, first published 1980).

Devine, T. M., *Clearance and Improvement: Land, Power and People in Scotland 1700 – 1900* (Edinburgh, 2006).

Devine, T. M., *The Scottish Nation 1700 – 2000* (London, 2000, first published 1999).

Ennew, Judith, *The Western Isles Today* (Cambridge, 1980).

Fenton, Alexander & Mulhern, Mark A., (editors), *A Swedish Field Trip to the Outer Hebrides, 1934* (Edinburgh, 2012).

Fenyő, Krisztina, *Contempt, Sympathy and Romance – Lowland Perceptions of the Highlands and the Clearances During the Famine Years, 1845 – 1855* (East Linton, 2000).

Fraser Darling, Frank, West Highland Survey: An Essay in Human Ecology (Oxford, 1955).

Geddes, Arthur, *The Isle of Lewis and Harris – A Study in British Community* (Edinburgh, 1955).

Gibson, Rosemary, *The Scottish Countryside: Its Changing Face* (Edinburgh, 2007).

Glendenning, Miles & Wade Martins, Susanna, *Buildings of the Land: Scotland's Farms 1750-2000* (Edinburgh, 2008).

Grigor, Iain Fraser, *Highland Resistance: The Radical Tradition in the Scottish North* (Edinburgh, 2000).

Harper, Marjory, *Emigration from Scotland between the Wars: Opportunity or Exile?* (Manchester, 2009, first published Manchester 1998).

Harper, Marjory, *Adventurers and Exiles: The Great Scottish Exodus* (London, 2003).

Harper, Marjory, *Scotland No More? The Scots Who Left Scotland in the Twentieth Century* (Edinburgh, 2012).

Hunter, James, *The Making of the Crofting Community* (Edinburgh, 1982, first published 1976).

Hunter, James, *The Claim of Crofting: The Scottish Highlands and Islands, 1930 – 1990* (Edinburgh, 1991).

Hunter, James, *On the Other Side of Sorrow – Nature and People in the Scottish Highlands* (Edinburgh, 1995).

Hunter, James, *Last of the Free – A Millennial History of the Highlands and Islands of Scotland* (Edinburgh, 1999).

Hunter, James, *Scottish Exodus: Travels Among a Worldwide Clan* (Edinburgh, 2005).

Hunter, James, *From the Low Tide of the Sea to the Highest Mountain Tops* (Isle of Lewis, 2012).

Hunter, James, *Set Adrift Upon The World: The Sutherland Clearances* (Edinburgh, 2015).

Hunter, Janet, *A Future for North Harris: The North Harris Trust* (Isle of Harris, 2007)

Hutchinson, Roger, *The Soapman* (Edinburgh, 2003).

Islands Book Trust, *The Land Struggle in Skye and Lewis – Aimhreit an Fhearainn* (Isle of Lewis, 2011).

Jones, David S. D., *The Sporting Estates of the Outer Hebrides Past and Present: An Illustrated History* (Salisbury, 2008).

Lawson, Bill, *Croft History Isle of Lewis, Volume 14 for Comann Eachdraidh na Pairc* (Stornoway, 2007).

Lawson, Bill, *Lewis in History and Legend – the East Coast* (Edinburgh, 2011).

Lawson, Bill, *Harris in History and Legend* (Edinburgh, 2008).

Leneman, Leah, *Fit for Heroes? Land Settlement in Scotland after World War I* (Aberdeen, 1989).

MacAskill, John, *We Have Won the Land – The Story of the Purchase by the Assynt Crofters' Trust of the North Lochinver Estate* (Stornoway, 1999).

MacColl, Allan W., *Land, Faith and the Crofting Community: Christianity and Social Criticism in the Highlands of Scotland 1843 – 1893* (Edinburgh, 2006).

Macdonald, Angus & Patricia, *The Hebrides – An Aerial View of a Cultural Landscape* (Edinburgh, 2010).

Macdonald, Christine, *Lewis – The Story of an Island* (Isle of Lewis, 1998, first published, 1982).

Macdonald, Donald, *Lewis – A History of the Island* (London, 2004, first published 1978).

MacDonald, John, *An Trusadh: Memories of Crofting in the Ardveg* (Isle of Lewis, 2013).

Macdonald, Sharon, *Reimagining Culture: Histories, Identities and the Gaelic Renaissance* (Oxford, 1997).

Mackenzie, A., Fiona, D., *Places of Possibility – Property, Nature and Community Land Ownership* (Chichester, 2013).

Mackenzie, Alexander, *The History of the Highland Clearances* (Aberdeen, 1883).

MacLean, Malcolm & Carrell, Christopher (editors), *From the Land As an Fhearann – Clearance, Conflict and Crofting: A Century of Images of the Scottish Highlands* (Stornoway, 1986).

Mather, Alexander S., *State-aided Land Settlement in Scotland, O'Dell Memorial Monograph no. 6, Department of Geography, University of Aberdeen* (Aberdeen, 1978).

Mathieson, Robert, *The Survival of the Unfittest – the Highland Clearances and the End of Isolation* (Edinburgh, 2000).

Miers, Mary, *The Western Seaboard: An Illustrated Architectural Guide* (Edinburgh, 2008).

Moisley, H. A., *Uig A Hebridean Parish* (1961).

National Museums Scotland, *Land and Legacy, Fonn 's Duthchas – The Scottish Highlands: A Contested Country* (Edinburgh, 2006).

Nicolson, Nigel, *Lord of the Isles* (Isle of Lewis, 2000; first published London, 1960).

Orr, Willie, *Deer Forests, Landlords and Crofters – The Western Highlands in Victorian and Edwardian Times* (Edinburgh, 1982).

Parman, Susan, *Scottish Crofters: A Historical Ethnography of a Celtic Village* (London, 2005, first published 1990).

Randall, John, *The Historic Shielings of Pàirc* (Isle of Lewis, 2017).

Richards, Eric, *The Highland Clearances* (Edinburgh, 2008, first published 2000).

Robertson, Iain J. M., *Landscapes of Protest in the Scottish Highlands after 1914: The Later Highland Wars* (Farnham, 2013).

Robson, Michael, *The Great Forest of Lewis* (Isle of Lewis, 2011).

Sawyers, June Skinner, *Bearing the People Away* (Canada, 2013).

Schama, Simon, *Landscape and Memory* (London, 1995).

Thompson, Francis, *The Western Isles* (London, 1988).

Thompson, Francis, *Harris and Lewis* (Newton Abbot, 1968).

Wightman, Andy, *Who Owns Scotland* (Edinburgh, 1997, first published 1996).

Wightman, Andy, *Scotland: Land and Power – The Agenda for Land Reform* (Edinburgh, 2000, first published, 1999).

Wightman, Andy, *The Poor Had No Lawyers – Who Owns Scotland (And How They Got it)* (Edinburgh, 2010).

Wilkie, Jim, *Metagama. A Journey from Lewis to the New World* (Edinburgh, 1987).

Withers, Charles W. J., *Gaelic Scotland: The Transformation of a Culture Region* (London, 1988).

Wylie, Gus, *Patterns of the Hebrides* (London, 1981).

ARTICLES AND PAMPHLETS:

Beckett, John, & Turner, Michael, 'End of the Old Order? F. M. L. Thompson, The Land Question, and the Burden of Ownership in England, c. 1880 – c. 1925', *Agricultural History Review*, volume 55, 2007.

Cameron, Ewen A., 'The Seven Men of Knoydart and the Scottish Highlands in the 1940s', *Transactions of the Gaelic Society of Inverness*, volume 62, 2001-2003.

Cameron, Ewen A., 'Unfinished Business: The Land Question and the Scottish Parliament', *Contemporary British History*, volume 15, number 1. (Spring 2001), pp. 83-114.

Cameron, Ewen A., 'Communication or Separation? Reactions to Irish Land Agitation and Legislation in the Highlands of Scotland, c. 1870 – 1910', *English Historical Review*, 120 (2005).

Cameron, Ewen A., 'The Scottish Highlands as a Special Policy Area, 1886 to 1965', *Rural History*, (1997) 8, 2, pp. 195-215.

Cameron, Ewen A., & Newby, Andrew, 'Alas, Skyemen are Imitating the Irish: A Note on Alexander Nicolson's "Little Leaflet" Concerning the Crofters' Agitation', *The Innes Review*, volume 55, number 1 (Spring, 2004).

Cameron, Ewen A., 'Setting the Heather on Fire: The Land Question in Scotland, 1850 – 1914', in Cragoe, Matthew & Readman, Paul, (editors), *The Land Question in Britain, 1750 – 1950* (Basingstoke, 2010).

Cameron, Ewen A., 'The Political Influence of Highland Landowners: A Reassessment', *Northern Scotland*, volume 14, 1994.

Cameron, Ewen A., 'They Will Listen to no Remonstrance: Land Raids in the Scottish Highlands, 1886 to 1914', *Scottish Economic and Social History*, 17, 1997.

Cameron, Ewen A., & Robertson, Iain J. M., 'Fighting and Bleeding for the Land: The Scottish Highlands and the Great War' in Macdonald, Catriona M. M., & McFarland, E. W., (editors), *Scotland and the Great War* (East Linton, 1999).

Cameron, Ewen A., 'The Scottish Highlands and the Conscience of the Nation, 1886 to 2003' in P. MacNeill (editor), *Papers from the Sixth Australian Celtic Conference, Sydney Series in Celtic Studies*, 9 (Sydney: University of Sydney, 2010).

Chambers, Bob, *Life on the Edge: Growing up in Steimreway – The Story of Chirsty Maggie Carmichael* (Isle of Lewis, 2011).

Coull, James R., The Importance of Fishing in the Napier Commission report of 1884, pp. 190-195, in William Ritchie, Jeffrey C. Stone and Alexander S. Mather (editors), *Essays for Professor R. E. H. Mellor* (Aberdeen, 1986).

Gibson, Rob, *The Promised Land* (Isle of Skye, 1974).

Gold, John R., & Gold, Margaret M., 'To be Free and Independent: Crofting, Popular Protest and Lord Leverhulme's Hebridean Development Projects, 1917 – 1925', *Rural History*, 7, 2, (1996).

Hunter, James, 'The Gaelic Connection: the Highlands, Ireland and Nationalism 1873 – 1922', *Scottish Historical Review*, 54, (1975).

Hunter, James, Crofting Works – But Could And Should Work Better, *The Sabhal Mòr Ostaig Lectures*, Lecture Number One, 1990.

Hunter, James, Moorland Without Crofters – *Second Angus Macleod Memorial Lecture*, 2005.

Jones, David, S. D., *The Eishken Estate* (Isle of Lewis, 2009).

Kennedy, Charles, Crofting and A European Future, *Sixth Angus Macleod Memorial Lecture*, 2009.

Kennedy, Kristine, Park – A Personal Perspective, *Fifth Angus Macleod Memorial Lecture*, 2008.

Lawrence, Jon, 'Forging a Peaceable Kingdom: War, Violence and Fear of Brutalisation in Post – First World War Britain', *Journal of Modern History*, volume 75, September 2003.

Lawson, Bill, *Lewis Families and How to Trace Them, Part 2 – Lochs* (Stornoway, 2005).

Lawson, Bill, The Clearances in Lewis – Truth or Myth? – *Third Angus Macleod Memorial Lecture*, 2006.

Macdonald, Fraser (editor), 'Colloqium – Susan Parman's Scottish Crofters: A Historical Ethnography of a Celtic Village', *Journal of Scottish Historical Studies*, 242, 2004.

Macleod, Mary, *Pairc – Old Enigmas and New Ideas* (Islands Book Trust, Island Notes number 33 – no date of publication).

Mather, Alexander S., 'The Rise and Fall of Government – assisted Land Settlement in Scotland', *Land Use Policy*, July 1985.

Mather, Alexander S., The Congested Districts Board for Scotland, in *Essays for Professor R. E. H. Mellor* (Aberdeen, 1986).

Mather, Alexander S., 'Government Agencies and Land Development in the Scottish Highlands: A Centenary Survey', *Northern Scotland*, number 8, 1988.

McCrone, David, & Morris, Angela, 'Lords and Heritages: The Transformation of the Great Lairds of Scotland' in Devine, T. M., (editor), *Scottish Elites* (Edinburgh, 1994).

McCrone, David, 'Towards a Principled Society: Scottish Elites in the Twentieth Century' in, Dickson, A. & Treble, J. H., (editors), *People and Society in Scotland*, volume 3. 1914 – 1990 (Edinburgh, 1992).

Meek, Donald, E., Charging at an Open Door? An Alternative View of Crofting History and Highland Development Since 1930 From the Gaelic Writings of the Reverend Dr T. M. Murchison (1907 – 1984), *Ninth Angus Macleod Memorial Lecture*, 2012.

Rennie, Agnes, Land Reform – Our Legacy From Generations Past, Creating Opportunities for Future Generations, *Seventh Angus Macleod Memorial Lecture*, 2010.

Robertson, Iain J. M., 'Governing the Highlands: The Place of Popular Protest in the Highlands of Scotland after 1918', *Rural History*, 8 (1997).

Robertson, Iain J. M., 'Land, People and Identity: Popular Protest in the Scottish Highlands after 1918' in Morris, R. J., & Kennedy, L., (editors), *Ireland and Scotland: Order and Disorder, 1600 – 2000* (Edinburgh, 2005).

Robertson, Iain J. M., 'The Role of Women in Social Protest in the Highlands of Scotland, c. 1880 – 1939', *Journal of Historical Geography*, xxiii (1997).

Rubinstein, William D, 'Britain's Elites in the Inter – War Period, 1918 – 1939: Decline or Continued Ascendancy?', *British Scholar*, volume 3, issue 1, September 2010.

Shaw, Donald, *The Idrigill Raiders* (Ullapool, 2010).

Shaw, Donald, *After the Highland Clearances: Reclaiming Lost Lands* (Ullapool, 2011).

Tindley, Annie, 'The System of Landlordism Supreme: David Lloyd George, the 5th Duke of Sutherland, and Highland Land Sales 1898 – 1919', *British Scholar*, volume 3, issue 1, September 2010.

Watt, Monique, *South Lochs in the Leverhulme Era – A Community in Crisis* (Isle of Lewis, 2012).

Wilson, Brian, The Future of Crofting – The case for Crofting Tenure, *Fourth Angus Macleod Memorial Lecture*, 2007.

Withers, Charles W. J., 'Rural Protest in the Highlands of Scotland and Ireland, 1859 – 1930' in Connolly, S. J., Houston, R. A., & Morris, R. J., (editors), *Conflict, Identity and Economic Development: Ireland and Scotland, 1600 – 1939* (Preston, 1995).

Withers, Charles W. J., 'Give us Land and Plenty of it; The Ideological Basis to Land and Landscapes in the Scottish Highlands', *Landscape History*, 12 (1990).

PUBLIC REPORTS:

Board of Agriculture for Scotland Annual Reports, 1913-1950.

Congested Districts Board Annual Reports, 1897-1912.

Crofters Commission Annual Reports, 1886-1912.

Scottish Land Court Reports, 1913-1939.

PARLIAMENTARY PAPERS:

PP 1851, XXVI, *Report to the Board of Supervision by Sir John McNeill on the Western Highlands and Islands* (McNeill report).

PP 1884, XXXIII-XXXVI, C 3980, *Report of the Commission of Inquiry into the Condition of the Crofters and Cottars in the Highlands and Islands of Scotland* (Napier Commission report, after its chairman, Lord Francis Napier).

Confidential report to the Secretary for Scotland on the condition of the Western Highlands and Islands, 1886. There is a copy of this on file AF67/401 in NRS – it is printed (by HMSO), not typed, and extends to 95 pages though the report is only 20 pages and the rest appendices. The report's author is Malcolm McNeill (see reference PP 1888 etc immediately below this one). It covers Skye; Barra, South Uist, North Uist, Harris; The Lews; Western Seaboard and Mull District. The current author has not been able to find out a great deal about this report (perhaps because of its confidential nature, the reason for which is not known)other than additional information in AF67/404 (this file contains the report – dated July 1890 – of the commissioners appointed to the inquiry and the reference is C. 6138. The commissioners are named: Spencer Walpole – Lieutenant Governor of the Isle of Man; Sir James King; Dugald Mackechnie; Commander Arthur M. Farquhar RN; John Wolfe Barry; and Malcolm McNeill); AF67/405 (a second report by the commissioners dated 1891, reference C. 6242 and covering the north coast of Sutherland and Caithness, plus the Orkney and Shetland Islands); and AF67/406 (notes of evidence taken by the commissioners appointed to the inquiry, containing 122 pages of witness statements).

PP 1888, LXXX, C. 5265, *Report to the Secretary for Scotland on the condition of the cottar population in the Lews.* (Fraser & McNeill report after its authors Alexander Fraser and Malcolm McNeill – both were Gaelic speakers).

PP 1895, XXXVIII-XXXIX, C 7668, *Royal Commission (Highlands and Islands 1892), Report and Evidence*, 1895 (Deer Forest Commission report).

PP 1902, LXXXIII, Cd 1327, *Report to the Secretary for Scotland by the Crofters Commission on the social condition of the people of Lewis in 1901, as compared with twenty years ago.*

PP 1905, *Report to the Secretary for Scotland by the Crofters Commission on the social condition of the people of Uist in 1903 as compared with twenty years ago.* There is a copy of this report in NRS on file AF67/411. It is printed and contains 125 pages plus 41 pages of appendices. The report is dated 30 July 1904 and is by David Brand, P. B. Macintyre and James N. Forsyth. It looks as though it may have been published/printed in 1905. The Crofters

Commission was asked in 1903 to produce the report. The printed report does not have a reference number.

PP 1917-18, XIV, Cd 8731, *Report of the Royal Commission on the Housing of the Individual Population of Scotland Rural and Urban* (Ballantyne Commission report, after its chairman, Sir Henry Ballantyne).

PP 1928, XI, Cmd 3110, *Report of the Committee on Land Settlement in Scotland* (Nairne Committee report, after its chairman, Sir John Gordon Nairne).

1944-45, V, Cmd 6577, *Report of the Scottish Land Settlement Committee* (Douglas Committee report, after its chairman, James Boyd Douglas).

1954, VIII, Cmd 9091, *Report of the Commission of Enquiry into Crofting Conditions* (Taylor Commission report, after its chairman, Thomas Murray Taylor).

2014, *Scottish Government report to the Scottish Parliament: Economic Condition of Crofting 2011-2014*. This is a report required by Section 51 of the Crofting Reform (Scotland) Act 2010. It was published on 19 December 2014 and is the second such report to have been produced.

OTHER REPORTS:

The Highlands and Islands of Scotland: a Review of the Economic Conditions with Recommendations for Improvement, Scottish Economic Committee, 1938 (Hilleary Committee report).

Land Use in the Highlands and Islands. Report submitted by the Advisory Panel of the Highlands and Islands to the Secretary of State for Scotland, 27 October 1964.

- ACKNOWLEDGEMENTS -

It has been quite an undertaking researching and producing this history of the complicated and drawn out Pairc Estate community buyout. A considerable number of individuals and organisations have contributed in a variety of ways. Without their input the book would not have been possible. It is a pity and a matter of personal regret to the author, however, that the previous owner of the estate and a couple of other individuals chose not to contribute. Had they done so then this may well have changed or modified some of my views and conclusions. However, for my part, I am satisfied that they were given a genuine opportunity to contribute. I feel that the conclusions I have reached are therefore fair and objective, based on the evidence and material available to me.

The Pairc Trust has been on hand to help whenever the author has required assistance. Otherwise it has allowed him to get on with the job. It has respected the author's independence in carrying out the work it commissioned from him to research and write a history of the buyout.

The author would like to thank all past and present directors of the Pairc Trust who have contributed to the study, but particularly the current chairman Angus McDowall and former vice chairman Steve Mortimore for their support and encouragement. John Randall, a previous director (and post holder) of the Pairc Trust, has also provided the author with much information and documentation.

The other person who I would particularly like to acknowledge for his time and assistance is Roy Shearer. He is now a retired solicitor in Edinburgh, and for much of the duration of the buyout he was the chief legal adviser to the Pairc Trust. The author has been impressed with Roy Shearer's measured views and opinions. However, it needs to be emphasised that, whilst a number of the author's conclusions may well be shared by Roy Shearer, they have been formulated by the author and are not a mouthpiece for the Pairc Trust's former legal adviser and representative.

I would also like to single out for special mention David Cameron of Tarbert on the Isle of Harris. He is a former chairman of Community Land Scotland and was also a key figure in the North Harris Estate community buyout. David Cameron mediated negotiations between the Pairc Trust and the previous Estate owner during 2013 and 2014. Without his input a voluntary transfer of the estate may not have happened or may well have taken even longer than it did. David Cameron has been very generous to the author with his time and views on the buyout. Again, the author would like to state that whilst some of David Cameron's views may be reflected in the text, the conclusions are those of the author and any overlap between the two is coincidental.

Various officials of Scottish Government, Highlands and Islands Enterprise, and Western Isles Council (Comhairle nan Eilean Siar) have also been extremely helpful in providing the author with information and documentation – which he would like to acknowledge. Sandra Holmes of HIE was a key figure throughout the buyout process, as was Calum Iain MacIver of the Comhairle.

The author would like to thank Jim Hunter for his preface which puts the Pairc Estate community buyout into a far wider context. Jim Hunter is, without doubt, in my view, the most authoritative voice on crofting history. His knowledge and understanding of community land ownership and land reform in Scotland are also formidable.

Last, but not least, the author's partner Shirley has been a constant source of support throughout the process of researching and writing this text.

Bob Chambers

- INDEX -